Thinking Quests

Thinking Quests

Extension and Enrichment Activities for Students

Book 2 Grades 4-8

by Lindy T. Redmond

PRUFROCK PRESS INC

Graphic design and production by James Kendrick and Christiane Kendrick
Illustrations on pages 33 and 52 by Justin W. Norris

Printed in the United States of America.

ISBN 1-882664-90-6

At the time of this book's publication, all facts and figures cited are the most current available. All telephone numbers, addresses, and Web site URLs are accurate and active. All publications, organizations, Web sites, and other resources exist as described in the book, and all have been verified. The author and Prufrock Press, Inc., make no warranty or guarantee concerning the information and materials given out by organizations or content found at Web sites, and we are not responsible for any changes that occur after this book's publication. If you find an error, please contact Prufrock Press, Inc. We strongly recommend to parents, teachers, and other adults that you monitor children's use of the Internet.

Prufrock Press, Inc.
P.O. Box 8813
Waco, Texas 76714-8813
(800) 998-2208
Fax (800) 240-0333
http://www.prufrock.com

This book is dedicated to the children:

To my sons, Kevin and Tim,
who have blessed our lives with love, laughter, and the meaning of life.

To my new "daughter" Emily,
who has blessed our lives with love, warmth, and grace.

To our special children, Madeleine, Catherine, Irina, Nathanael,
Anna, Haleigh, Emily, Micaela, Jemma, Erin, Megan, and Quinn,
who have blessed our lives with hugs, hide and seek, knock-knock jokes, silly faces, and giggles.

Special thanks to:

My husband Tom,
who continuously supports and encourages all of my endeavors,

Donald J. Treffinger,
whose expertise and friendship has made work become a pleasure,

and Christiane Kendrick,
whose skillfulness and patience has made straw turn into gold.

Table of Contents

Bugs

Sports and Outdoor Activities

Parks and Forests

Weather

Appendices

From the Author

Dear Educator,

Authors speak from the heart. We write because we have a belief, a personal theory that we have internalized, and it has been tested and reconfirmed throughout our lives. This book is written by an experienced educator who has studied cognitive approaches to thinking, explored a variety of learning theories, and taught hundreds of children over the past 30 years. My personal preferences for learning strategies (hands-on learning, the use of critical and creative thinking, the teacher as a facilitator, and the use of activities that encourage students to create their own knowledge) are woven throughout this text.

As the world continues to change at a rapid pace, educators can no longer teach and train young people for a specific occupation, especially since new jobs are appearing daily. We must teach them how to think, solve problems, see multiple options and alternative solutions, build teamwork, and develop a plan of action. It is difficult to imagine the occupations that will be needed in the future. In order to compete for jobs and advance society, learners need to be able to generate a variety of options (*fluency*), shift from one train of thought to another (*flexibility*), contribute to original ideas (*elaboration*), and create novel, unique ideas (*originality*). These concepts—fluency, flexibility, elaboration, and originality—are the basic tenets of creative thinking and creative problem solving, and they are incorporated into the activities within *Thinking Quests: Extension and Enrichment Activities for Students in Grades 4–8*.

This book is designed to provide a series of theme-based activities that are related to each of the content areas and aligned to educational standards so that student learners can begin asking themselves, "What if . . ." It is my hope that by using this book, learners of all ages will build a foundation for accepting challenges as opportunities, rather than problems.

Lindy

Before You Begin

Overview

Following the educational ideas of Jerome Bruner (1965) and John Dewey, learners should discover principles (underlying key concepts about a content area) on their own and construct meaning for themselves. This idea, known as *discovery learning*, encourages students to take an active role in the learning process as it encourages them to integrate new ideas, concepts, and principles with their current knowledge base. If student learners are involved and complete activities that reinforce principles they have already learned, then their understanding and proficiency grow in a spiral fashion (they increase their depth and understanding of the topic under study).

How to Use This Book

As with any book of enrichment activities, there are a variety of ways the information can be used with student learners. This text is separated into six different themes for students in grades 4–8 (Animals, Flowering Plants, Bugs, Sports and Outdoor Activities, Parks and Forests, and Weather). Each theme has 10 stand-alone activities, which get progressively more advanced within each theme; however, the activities may be completed in any order. The final activity allows students to make connections among the various activities in each theme. As the difficulty within each theme increases, the role of the teacher may change. The beginning activities allow teachers to take a facilitative approach by encouraging the learner to discover new knowledge and make connections to past knowledge. At this level, students should be able to complete the activities independently, without teacher assistance (Vygotsky, 1978). As students progress through a theme, they may need more scaffolded instruction (teacher assistance or guidance). Some activities, depending on learner needs and abilities, may require direct instruction from a teacher, parent, or skilled other. The progression in mentally challenging activities, which are matched to students' learning needs, help to guide the growth of student learning (Piaget, 1973).

Have student learners read the directions for each activity. There are many correct answers for most of the activities, and only a few have definite, accurate responses. Encourage student learners to look in the answer section for specific answers, and feel free to add your own creative responses.

As students are guiding and constructing meaning for themselves, encourage them to use the Tracking Chart on the next page. Because the activities do not have to be followed in the

Tracking Chart

This is your Tracking Chart. This chart keeps track of all the theme activities you complete. Find the row that names the theme and the number of the activity you completed. As you finish activities, either color in one box or put one of your favorite small stickers in the box. That will help you keep track of the activities you have completed.

	1	2	3	4	5	6	7	8	9	10
Animals										
Flowering Plants										
Bugs										
Sports and Outdoor Activities										
Parks and Forests										
Weather										

sequence they are presented in the text, the chart can be used by students to help them keep track of the activities they have completed. Using the chart in this manner helps to reinforce the idea that students are creating their own knowledge by allowing them to take an active role in the learning process.

As educators, it is important to provide a challenge to student learners—providing tasks that are within the mental range of abilities for each learner in order to maintain interest and motivation (Pintrich & Schunk, 1996; Vygotsky, 1978). Because some activities are more complex than others, adjustments may need to be made depending on student learner needs. Learner needs are individual, and one lesson cannot meet the needs of all students. For this reason, feel free to use manipulatives or make other accommodations. If an activity that requires writing a story is too difficult, then modifications could include a student using a tape recorder to tell his or her story, or a teacher, parent, or skilled other could write down the student's words. To adjust activities for students who need more complexity, completing research, locating information on the Internet, or creating a model that illustrates the ideas in the selected activity are options that encourage them to integrate what they have learned into their current understanding of a theme. Making adjustments such as these should not decrease the level of cognitive challenge presented to the student learner, but rather should make accommodations for the type of output (end product) he or she will produce (Maker & Nielson, 1995).

Cognitive Abilities

If everyone thinks, why teach thinking skills? Although learners at all ability levels use their mental abilities, "many students . . . are unable to do the kind of thinking and problem solving that their schoolwork requires" (Nickerson, 1987, p. 441). Thinking can be categorized in many different ways. *Thinking Quests* focuses on the development of creative and critical thinking skills for learners in grades 4–8. Examples of these thinking skills include: comparing, summarizing, observing, classifying, interpreting, criticizing, looking for assumptions, imagining, collecting and organizing data, hypothesizing, applying facts and principles in a new situation, decision making, designing projects or investigations, and coding (Raths, Wasserman, Jonas, & Rothstein, 1986).

Theory and research on creativity, critical thinking, and Creative Problem Solving (CPS) by many scholars have influenced educational practice. Early pioneers, such as Guilford (1977), Osborn (1953), Parnes (1967), and Torrance (1962), called for the need to address creativity in education by offering practical insights into assessing and nurturing creativity and CPS. In more recent years, Isaksen, Treffinger, and others (e.g., Isaksen, Dorval, & Treffinger, 2000; Treffinger, Isaksen, & Dorval, 2000; Treffinger & Nassab, 2000) have advanced our understanding of these processes and their implications for teaching and learning. These researchers have described many tools and skills that can be used to assist learners as they generate a multitude of options (*fluency*), shift from one idea to another (*flexibility*), add to original concepts (*elaboration*), and create novel, unique ideas (*originality*). In using these tools, students learn how to focus critically and select the most appropriate choice(s).

Creative Thinking

Creativity is the production of work that is novel, original, high in quality, and deemed appropriate by standards established by peers (Sternberg & Williams, 2002). The creative process often begins with the generation of new ideas, often referred to as *creative thinking*. This kind of thinking requires the use of deferred judgment (not judging ideas until the end). In order to get a lot of different ideas, the process of generating encourages learners to (1) identify many ideas or possibilities, (2) consider unusual or unique possibilities, (3) take alternative or nontraditional points-of-view, and (4) elaborate or expand on ideas already in use.

Critical Thinking

Critical thinking encourages learners to consciously and purposely focus their thoughts and energy to find a solution to a problem (Halpern, 1998; Paul, 1995). Therefore, for learners to understand what they are taught, they need to be aware of and in control of their own thinking about a topic, also known as *metacognitive awareness*. This type of thinking also requires the use of affirmative judgment. Critical thinkers focus on and deliberately select the best idea from a variety of options and do so in a constructive or affirmative way. As learners focus in on a topic, they (1) analyze and organize the ideas, (2) fine-tune and develop the ideas further, (3) prioritize them in an order they like best, and (4) select the best option(s).

Paul's (1995) assumptions surrounding educational practices that encourage critical thinking include:

- Students learn *what* to think only as they learn how to think.

- One gains knowledge *only* through thinking.

- The process of education is the process of each student gathering, analyzing, synthesizing, applying, and assessing information for him- or herself.

- Classes with much student talk focused on live issues is a better sign of learning than quiet classes focused on a passive acceptance of what the teacher says.

- Students gain significant knowledge only when they value it.

- Information should be presented so as to be understandable from the point of view of the learner, hence continually related to the learner's experiences and point of view.

- Superficial learning is often mislearning and stands as an obstacle to deeper understanding.

- Depth is more important than coverage.

- Students can often provide correct answers, repeat definitions, and apply formulas while not understanding those answers, definitions, and formulas.

- Students learn best by working together with other students, actively debating and exchanging ideas. (p. 277, emphasis in original)

Many of the activities in this book encourage students to generate a list of possible scenarios, choices, or ideas. In creating these lists and sharing their ideas with their peers, student learners are working on increasing their abilities to use a variety of skills and tools. After learners propose their ideas, they can work in small groups, as a whole class, or with a skilled other to select criteria and judge their responses. This continuous connection between idea generating and solution finding reinforces the use of the skills and tools students need to be successful creative and critical thinkers.

Thinking Skills and Learning Tools

Proficiency in thinking skills and learning tools enables learners to grasp material at a faster rate, connect past knowledge with new knowledge for comprehensive meaning, and organize information for quick recall. *Skills* are levels of performance or proficiencies of which a person is capable. Mozart possessed the skill of composing classical music. *Tools* are the equipment needed to practice or apply the skills. Mozart used the tools of the piano, staff paper, and a writing utensil to compose his masterpieces. If we think of the game of bowling, the actual ability of being a bowler is a skill. The ball, bowling alley, bowling shoes, and bowling pins are all tools that help the bowler become more proficient. The definitions of the specific skills and tools are listed below. The alignment of the skills and tools used for each activity are listed in the Appendix.

Applying Facts and Principles in a New Situation: (Skill) A thinking skill required when a situation requires previous knowledge (learned principles, rules, generalizations, or laws) and students apply that knowledge within a new situation. This typically includes predicting what will occur using previous knowledge and facts in a new context.

Classifying: (Skill) Classifying is looking at a group of items and sorting them into specific categories of likeness. This involves examining a group of objects and putting them together into groups based on similar characteristics.

Collecting and Organizing Data: (Tool and skills) Student-centered activities that allow the learner to formulate his or her own questions, gather relevant information, examine materials, and integrate the findings. This skill may include additional tools, such as interviewing and forming questionnaires or surveys. While comparing data, students see a variety of objects, processes, and people. As more data is collected, students begin to organize the ideas into a meaningful whole via a report, presentation, or computer presentation.

Comparing and Contrasting: (Skill) Observing the similarities and differences of items and determining the relationships between one another. This skill often considers points of agreement and disagreement.

Criticizing: (Skill) Using standards to guide our ideas and beliefs, criticizing is the judgment against a pre-identified quality or benchmark. It includes a critical evaluation of specific criteria deemed important by the critic and identifies both aspects of worth and deficiencies.

Decision Making: (Skill) Similar to Applying Facts and Principles in a New Situation, decision making focuses on the role values take in specific contexts. Prompts, such as "What should happen to . . . ?" or "Why do you think . . . ?" encourage students to view values (desires, hopes, and purposes) as being equally relevant and important when considering social and personal matters.

Designing Projects or Investigations: (Skill) A large-scale assignment that includes many smaller activities and may stretch across several weeks. Students typically outline the project before they begin. When working in groups, roles (recorder, researcher, etc.) may be parceled out among those involved and due dates established.

Hypothesizing: (Skill) The process of suggesting a possible solution to a problem. Hypothesis are efforts, hunches, or guesses that offer explanations for how or why something works. Also considered educated guesses, hypotheses are guides to use while attempting to find the unknown.

Imagining: (Skill) The formation of an idea that is not in the present or the past. Generally considered a creative ability, imagining allows one to create mental images or representations that others cannot see or experience.

Interpreting: (Skill) Expression of the meaning an object or idea has and represents. Interpreting involves both the taking meaning out of or giving meaning to our personal experiences. This typically includes supporting ideas, such as graphs, charts, tables, photographs, stories, and so forth. Interpretations also include the reactions to experiences (vacations, accidents, family get-togethers).

Looking for Assumptions: (Skill) Something taken for granted and not generally questioned. Assumptions are generally constructed when investigations cannot be made to determine the truth or falsity of a statement. Whenever conclusions (critical judgments) are made, assumptions are made at the same time.

Observing: (Skill) Observing, noting, watching, perceiving, and determining what occurs over a specific amount of time. This requires close attention to details and watching with a purpose in mind. Observing can include focusing on minute details, on a procedure, or both.

Summarizing: (Skill) Stating in a concise or brief manner the information previously presented. It identifies the main points or ideas of a text.

Concept Formation

As student learners begin to understand and make their own categories, they are forming *concepts*. These categories may be as simple as classifications of people, animals, cars, or houses. Much of what educators teach are the skills and tools needed for students to be able to put new information into pre-existing concepts (comedy, spicy, height, latitude, rectangles) or teaching students how to form new, original concepts. The formation of these concepts may seem obvious to adults; however, research by Keil (1999) has suggested that students learn and form concepts in a variety of ways. It is for this reason that educators must be knowledgeable about the various approaches they can take to assist student learners. The specific activities in *Thinking Quests* are designed to help students expand their current concepts on themes discussed regularly within the classroom. Each theme can be used as an independent unit or they can be used as a large interdisciplinary unit, which allows students to identify generalizations common across all the themes and the impact each theme has on our ecosystem. At the end of each theme is a final activity for students to reflect on the ideas and concepts gained throughout the activities. These may be used as a culminating activity or as notes to refer back to when identifying the interrelationships among the various themes (Johnsen, 1997). See the Appendix for more information regarding the concepts and learning objectives for each unit and activity.

Learning Standards

In the national effort to develop thinking skills among student learners, statewide and national tests require students to remember specific materials and analyze and evaluate material. Because of such efforts, state and national standards have been developed to guide the development of students at each grade level. Currently, 49 of the 50 states have written and adopted state standards (Mid-Continent Research in Education and Learning, 2002). Many school districts are focusing on raising student performance. In a recent project, I helped review the standards for 33 states and found the concepts among the standards were similar, even though the actual wording differed.

Each activity in this text is aligned to national standards within the core content areas: math, science, geography, social studies, and language arts. These standards have been designed and approved by the National Council of Teachers of Mathematics (2000), the National Academy of Sciences (2001), the National Council for the Social Studies (1994), the National Geographic Society (Geography Education Standards Project, 1994), and the National Council of Teachers of English (1996). See the Appendix for specific alignment between the unit activities and the national standards.

Cognitive Challenge

The standards discussed in Appendix 1 are general in nature and focus on cognitive goals. Following Gronlund's (1991) emphasis, *Thinking Quests* encourages learners to focus on overarching concepts and ideas, rather than specific measurable actions. Students will gather the objectives from each specific material and should track the activities they have completed using the Tracking Chart. At the same time, educators should help student learners to understand that the skills and tools they are using are similar across the themes, thus encouraging students to think across the various content areas.

A Personal Challenge

In 1997, the Work Group of the American Psychological Association's Board of Educational Affairs created Learner-Centered Principles that encourage students to become more engaged in their own learning process while their teacher or parent takes on the role of a facilitator. These 14 principles encourage personal responsibility, pursuance of personal goals, linking new information to existing knowledge, and internal learner motivation. Additionally, the principles stress the importance of presenting material to the learner at the appropriate developmental level, setting high standards, and introducing it in an interesting manner. It is my belief that the presentation of the material, the excitement of the facilitator, and the differentiation of the activities all entice the desire for learning. The philosophy embedded in these principles is intermingled throughout these theme activities.

My challenge to you as practitioners is to make learning rewarding, fulfilling, and thrilling! In your quest to create a passion for thinking within all learners, actively involve them in each challenge. Use the following activities as a springboard for enhancing curiosity and encouraging exploration.

References

Bruner, J. (1965). *Toward a theory of instruction*. New York: Morrow.

Geography Education Standards Project. (1994). *Geography for life: National geography standards 1994*. Washington, DC: National Geographic Research and Exploration.

Gronlund, N. E. (1991). *How to write and use instructional objectives* (4th ed.). Englewood Cliffs, NJ: Prentice-Hall.

Guilford, J. P. (1977). *Way beyond the IQ*. Buffalo, NY: Bearly Limited.

Halpern, D. F. (1998). Teaching critical thinking for transfer across domains: Dispositions, skills, structure, training, and metacognitive monitoring. *American Psychologist, 53*, 449–455.

Isaksen, S. G., Dorval, K. B., & Treffinger, D. J. (2000). *Creative approaches to problem solving* (2nd ed.). Dubuque, IA: Kendall/Hunt.

Johnsen, S. K. (1997). Writing interdisciplinary standards. In S. K. Johnsen & B. Hay (Eds.), *Interdisciplinary curriculum by design* (pp. 2–21). Waco, TX: Baylor University's Interdisciplinary Problem Solving Conference.

Keil, F. C. (1999). Cognition, content, and development. In M. Bennett (Ed.), *Developmental psychology* (pp. 165–184). Philadelphia, PA: Psychology Press.

Maker, C. J., & Nielson, A. B. (1995). *Teaching models in education of the gifted*. Austin, TX: PRO-ED.

Mid-Continent Research in Education and Learning (McREL). (2002). *Standards at McREL*. Retrieved July 17, 2002, from http://www.mcrel.com/standards/index.asp.

National Academy of Sciences (NAS). (2001). *National science education standards*. Washington, DC: National Academy Press.

National Council for the Social Studies (NCSS). (1994). *Expectations of excellence: Curriculum standards for social studies*. Silver Spring, MD: Author.

National Council of Teachers of English (NCTE). (1996). *Standards for the English language arts*. Newark, DE: International Reading Association.

National Council of Teachers of Mathematics (NCTM). (2000). *Principles and standards for school mathematics*. Reston, VA: Author.

Nickerson, R. S. (1987). Why teach thinking? In J. B. Baron & R. J. Sternberg (Eds.), *Teaching thinking skills: Theory and practice* (pp. 27–37). New York: Freeman.

Osborn, A. F. (1953). *Applied imagination*. New York: Charles Scribner's Sons.

Parnes, S. J. (1967). *Creative behavior guidebook*. New York: Charles Scribner's Sons.

Paul, R. (1995). *Critical thinking: How to prepare students for a rapidly changing world*. Santa Rosa, CA: Foundation for Critical Thinking.

Piaget, J. (1973). *Main trends in psychology*. London: George Allen & Unwin.

Pintrich, P. R., & Schunk, D. H. (1996). *Motivation in education: Theory, research, and application*. Columbus, OH: Merrill.

Raths, E. L., Wasserman, S., Jonas, A., & Rothstein, A. (1986). *Teaching for thinking: Theory, strategies, and activities for the classroom.* New York: Teachers College Press.

Sternberg, R. J. & Williams, W. M. (2002). *Educational psychology.* Boston: Allyn and Bacon.

Torrance, E. P. (1962). *Guiding creative talent.* Englewood Cliffs, NJ: Prentice-Hall.

Treffinger, D. J., Isaksen, S. G., & Dorval, K. B. (2000). *Creative problem solving: An introduction* (3rd ed.). Waco, TX: Prufrock Press.

Treffinger, D. J., & Nassab, C. A. (2000). *Thinking tools lessons.* Waco, TX: Prufrock Press.

Vygotsky, L. S. (1978). *Mind in society: The development of higher psychological processes.* Cambridge, MA: Harvard University Press.

Work Group of the American Psychological Association's Board of Educational Affairs. (1997). *Learner-centered psychological principles.* New York: American Psychological Association.

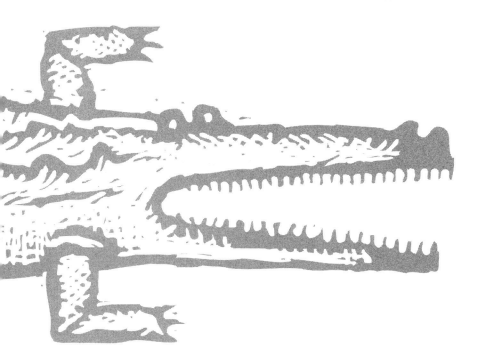

Perform a Silent Role

Talented actors are able to create stories, display emotions, and demonstrate the events of a specific situation without using words. These types of actors are called *pantomimes*. Famous pantomimes in the movies were Charlie Chaplin and Buster Keaton. When watching a pantomime, you may see the actor shuffle his feet, drop his head, and droop his shoulders to show the feeling of sadness. Or, you may see an actress arch her eyebrows, open her eyes wide, open her mouth, and raise her hands to her face to show surprise. The only trick is that pantomimes don't talk or make any noises when they perform. Often times, pantomimes exaggerate their gestures and facial expressions, making them larger than normal. In expressing the feelings of a character, audiences are able to understand a pantomime's intent.

Directions

This activity will require that you take on the role of a pantomime. Feel free to play this game with your parents or friends. In order to play, you will need to think of an animal. Consider the behavioral characteristics of the animal: How does this animal move? What does it eat? Where does it live? How does it act around other animals? Then, act out this animal using gestures and facial expressions to let your peers guess what animal you are enacting. The first person to guess correctly is the next one to act out an animal.

If you pantomime something that no one can guess, then make the animal's sound to help your peers guess what you are acting out. If they still cannot guess the animal you are pantomiming, then select another animal and take another turn.

Remember to:

- Use facial expressions: arch your eyebrows, grit your teeth, wiggle your ears.
- Use your entire body: arms, legs, head, neck, and torso.
- Move your body using the same movements as the animal: sway from side to side, jump up and down, squat down on the floor.
- Example: slow, slithering, crawling movements along the ground with your tongue flicking in and out would suggest a snake.

Try:
Elephant
Monkey
Crab
Penguin
Shark
Iguana
Frog

Thinking Quests

- Research five different types of animal groups (amphibians, birds, fish, mammals, or reptiles). Then, act out the various animals. Before you begin your pantomime, tell your audience the group to which your animal belongs.

- With your peers, create a list of 20 different animals. Write each name on an index card. Form two teams. Have the first player select a card and keep the name of the animal hidden. Then, pantomime the animal for his or her team. If the team guesses the name of the animal correctly, then they receive a point. Take turns pantomiming the animals by switching between the two teams. If a team cannot guess the correct animal name, then they do not receive a point. Continue until all the cards are used. The team with the most points wins. You can also select winners for best actor or actress for each team.

It's Time to Classify

Scientists have organized all living things into a classification system. Animals are just one kingdom of a classification system called *the five kingdoms*. The animal kingdom has five categories called *classes*: amphibia (amphibians), aves (birds), fish, mammalia (mammals), and reptilia (reptiles). These animals have been grouped together because they have similar biological and physical characteristics.

Directions

List the characteristics of each class of animals. Specific ideas to consider include: Where does this animal live (environment, climate)? How does this animal breathe (respire)? What type of support system does this animal have (skeleton, cartilage)? How does this animal react to other stimuli (animals, the environment)? How does it eat and digest food? How does it move? How does it protect itself? How does it reproduce? How does it care for its young? Is it warm- or cold-blooded? List the characteristics of each class below the name. Then, using the list of words in the box below, provide examples of each class. You might get some books from the library to help you or search the Internet.

pike	frog	owl	ostrich	eel	toad
crocodile	blue jay	desert tortoise	elephant	wolf	
salamander	rattlesnake	bison	sea horse		

Amphibians	Reptiles	Mammals	Birds	Fish
_____	_____	_____	_____	_____
_____	_____	_____	_____	_____
_____	_____	_____	_____	_____

15

Thinking Quests

- Make a list of 20 different animals, a minimum of 4 animals from each class, and compare your list with a friend. Look over your combined list and make a classification system by separating the animals into groups from different ecological regions: arctic, tundra, plains, forest, mountains, deserts, semiarid highlands, sierras, tropics, temperate. The North American Commission for Environmental Cooperation's Web site (http://www.cec.org/pubs_info_resources/publications/ enviro_conserv/ecomaps.cfm?varlan=English) may be helpful.

- Review the lists you created and list at least five statements for the following questions: How are the animals in each class similar? How are the animals in each class different? What characteristics do all animals have in common?

- Using the lists you created above, create your own classification system. For example, try classifying the animals by speed (fast, medium, slow) and determine the specific speeds that would place them into each category. Or, classify the animals by their appearance (most attractive, average, and least attractive). Share your results with friends. Do they agree? Why or why not? Consider why people all over the world use the five-kingdom classification system.

Recreate a Shape

Animals take many different forms. When you think about all the different kinds of birds that are on our planet, each one has a different function. Some birds eat nuts and berries, others eat fish, while others eat insects. The specific features of animals change depending on what they eat. For example, the woodpecker eats insects from trees and has a small, pointy beak. A pelican, on the other hand, has a large, scoop-like beak so it can gather fish from the ocean. Even birds that live in the water take different forms. Ducks and flamingos have different body shapes: One has long legs, the other has short ones for swimming.

Materials

- 4 pieces of paper that are the same size
- crayons or markers
- scissors
- 4 envelopes

Directions

1. Draw a different animal on each piece of paper. Make sure the animal takes up the entire piece of paper.
2. Select one drawing and cut it into 10–12 different puzzle pieces. For more of a challenge, try cutting the picture into smaller pieces.
3. Put your puzzle pieces into an envelope labeled with the animal's name. Follow the same steps for your other pictures.
4. Now, select one of your puzzles and put the picture back together. Have a friend try your puzzle.
5. What made some puzzles easy? What made others hard? What helped you to finish the puzzle? Did you think about the shapes of the animals? Did you think about the original shape of the paper? Did you match colors in the puzzle pieces?

Thinking Quests

- Fold at least 10 index cards into three equal parts. Draw a different animal on each card. When you draw each animal, put the head and neck on the right third, the body and arms on the center third, and the legs and tail on the left third. Cut the cards apart on the folds. Then, mix and match the animal bodies to create new, unique animals.

- What would you name an animal with a giraffe's neck, a monkey's body, and a duck's feet? After considering the characteristics you identified in the earlier Animal activities, what conclusions can you form about this new animal? Where would it live? What would it eat? How would it move? How would it care for its young? Select two of your mixed animals and write a paragraph about what makes these animals special.

- What animal do you like the most? What animals do you like least? What would happen if you took one part of each animal and combined it into a new animal, for example, an elephant with a giraffe's neck? What would your life be like if you had this animal as a pet? Write a story that tells what a normal day would be like with this pet.

Animal Antics

When you think of your friends, you can think about the person who is the friendliest, the funniest, the smartest, the fastest runner, the most creative, the best artist, or even the person with the most freckles. These are qualities or characteristics that each of us has, and, sometimes, there are certain characteristics that stand out or make us unique. Animals also have specific characteristics. For example, some animals are very muscular. Others, like the zebra or python, have special markings. And others make particular sounds or have unique body parts.

Directions

What animal(s) comes to mind when you think of these words? Write the animal's name on the line. Could there be more than one correct answer?

1. milk _____

2. stripes _____

3. mane _____

4. pouch _____

5. trunk _____

6. wise _____

7. long neck _____

8. America's bird _____

9. laughing _____

10. New York _____

11. man's best friend _____

12. carried mail _____

Thinking Quests

- Think about the animals you listed above. What are some of the specific characteristics of each animal? Use these characteristics to write riddles for 10 different animals. For example:

    Question: What animal flies in the air but is not a bird?
    Answer: A flying fish.

    Knock-knock jokes may be fun to make, as well. Use your jokes to make your own Animal Riddle Book.

- Select a rhyming-word family. Then, come up with another word that rhymes with your first word. For example, "He keeps *tryin'* to roar like a *lion*." Come up with a way you can use the two words together in a sentence. Make a list of 10 rhyming names using animals. Nursery rhymes, like "Hickory, Dickory Dock," are made using similar types of rhymes. Construct your own nursery rhymes. They can be about any topic: school, summer, sports, animals, your family, and so forth.

A New Ending

Predicting—using your imagination to think about what is going to happen next—encourages you to suppose and hypothesize. In thinking about a story from different points of view and considering different outcomes, we can change our previous ideas and beliefs. What would happen if you heard the fairy tale "Cinderella" from the prince's perspective? Or if you interviewed all of the characters in "Red Riding Hood"? Do you think you would hear the same things again and again? Would everyone's ideas on what happened be the same?

Directions

This activity asks you to pretend that the events in the story "The Three Little Pigs" have changed. Predict and write a new ending based on the facts that you know from the story so the ending you create could come true. Consider each idea separately. Feel free to add changes of your own.

- The first pig had a brick house?
- They all had brick houses?
- The wolf were friendly?
- The brick house blew down?
- There were five pigs?
- They were not pigs, but elephants instead?

Thinking Quests

- Select another well-known story. Make a list of five events that would change the original tale. Let your friend read the original story and predict outcomes that could occur based upon your generated list.

- Change a fairy tale into a story with factual information about the various animal characters. How does the story change? What things stay the same? Often times, we give animals human characteristics, personalities, or emotions. This is called *personification*. Why do you think fairy tales use animals in this way? Explain your answers.

20 Questions

This game asks you to look closely at animals. To play, you will need to think of an animal. Do not share the name of it with anyone. Then, thinking to yourself, remember the characteristics of this animal. Some questions you could ask yourself include:

- Where does this animal live?
- What does it eat?
- What size is it?
- Does it have special markings?
- Does it make a particular noise or sound?
- Is it found in more than one country?
- When does it sleep?
- Is the animal still living, or is it extinct?
- To what category (mammal, bird, fish, amphibians, reptiles)does it belong?
- How are the males and females similar and different?
- What is the animal's life span?
- How does it care for its young?

Directions

Play this game with a friend or in teams. One person picks an animal to be the special animal, and the other person or team asks questions to guess what it is. The questions must be asked in a way that the response can only be "Yes" or "No." If the animal is guessed correctly before 20 questions are asked, then the guesser(s) wins and the winner thinks of a new animal. If more than 20 questions are asked, then a new animal should be chosen.

Thinking Quests

- Try playing this game using animals from certain continents or geographic regions. If you play using the continent of Antarctica, then you may need to be specific on the characteristics among the different types of penguins.

- Make your own classification game based on the questions above. Design your own rules and make your own playing cards/board. Consider focusing your game on an ecological region or type of animal. Share your game with your friends.

"Oh, Give Me a Home"

"Oh, give me a home, where the buffalo roam,
And the deer and the antelope play.
Where seldom is heard, a discouraging word,
And the skies are not cloudy all day."

The song "Home on the Range" identifies characteristics of the environment or living conditions of what prairie life used to be like. It discusses the types of animals, the climate, and the general features of this habitat. A *habitat* is a place where certain organisms, in this case, animals, are likely to live and grow up. The specific area in the habitat where an animal lives is called its *niche*. Habitats typically include many different kinds of niches: ponds, rivers, forests, grasslands, and so forth.

Directions

Identify the characteristics of the niche and habitat for two different animals in each of the ecological regions below. Draw a picture that illustrates the difference between niche and habitat for three of the animals you identified.

arctic	tundra	taiga plains	forest	mountains	deserts
semiarid highlands		sierras		tropics	temperate

Thinking Quests

• Consider one habitat from above and list at least five animals from each phyla that live there. Then, identify their niches. Draw a map of your habitat and identify each animal's niche. Do you notice any patterns in how the animals live together in the habitat? What things do they have in common? How are they different?

• Animals that live in the same habitat often depend on one another for survival and nourishment. Looking at the map you constructed, identify the different food web patterns that occur in your habitat. What types of animals search for food within their niche? What animals search for food outside their niche? Are niches for animals the same size? Explain your answers.

What If . . .

Often times, good things can come from unexpected ideas. Some of our greatest inventions came to the minds of inventors when they were trying to solve problems. Problem solving encourages creative and critical thinking. Consider the list below and discuss the various problems that may occur for at least three of these "What if . . ." statements. Then, identify an original idea you could invent to help solve one of the problems. Write a paragraph about the function of your invention. What are its specific characteristics? How would it work? Why would it be needed? How much would it cost?

- What might happen if animals could talk?
- What might happen if all people owned four cats and four dogs?
- If you could be an animal, what animal would you be and why?
- How would life be different if dragons and unicorns were real?
- How would our world be different if dinosaurs returned?
- What might happen if animals were masters and we were their pets?
- What would happen if all of the tiny animals suddenly became huge and all of the big animals were transformed to being very small?
- What if . . . (make up your own).

Thinking Quests

- Select one of the ideas above and write a story about it. Use details to help describe the setting, the animals, and the problem. Using words that help your readers visualize what is going on will encourage people to read your story. Some authors use a suspenseful idea, also known as a *hook*, to lead readers through a story. Don't forget to share about how your invention helps to solve the problem.

- Create a picture book for a young child using the story you created. Write a simple text version of your story and illustrate it. Make a cover and share it with students in a younger class.

- Make an advertisement for your invention. Cut pictures out of magazines, draw your design, and write some basic information about your new product. Come up with a slogan or catch phrase that will help sell your idea. Share your idea with your friends.

Baby Names

There are different ways we name animals. All animals have a common name and a scientific name. The scientific name for dog is *canis familiaris*. Some animals names will change if it is a male or a female. For example, a horse may be called a *stallion* if it is a male and a *mare* if it is a female. If you have groups of animals together, the way they are talked about changes, too. You may see an *army* of caterpillars or a *school* of fish. When animals are babies, they are often known by unique names. For example, a baby cow is called a *calf*. Match the animals from column #1 to their baby names in column #2.

Column #1	Column #2
1. bear	_____ fawn
2. kangaroo	_____ gosling
3. cat	_____ puppy
4. sheep	_____ cub
5. dog	_____ lamb
6. deer	_____ foal
7. horse	_____ joey
8. goose	_____ kitten

Thinking Quests

• Use the list above as a starting point to research additional names of animals. Use reference books or the Internet (for example, http://www.zooish.com) to learn about different animal names. List the adult names, the baby names, the group names, and the different gender names for at least five different animals. Do some of the different animals use the same names? Why do you think these names are similar? Which names are the most common?

• Using the list you created above, survey your friends to see what animal names they know. What names are the most familiar? Which animal names are least familiar to the people you polled? Share your findings using a graphic and a poster.

Animal Generalizations

I f you had 5 minutes to tell someone about animals, what would you say? This is a difficult task, even for people who study animals for a living. When thinking about the theme of Animals, there are often important ideas we can take away that will help us to think about and remember how animals function. These important ideas are called *generalizations*. Generalizations are based on factual information or basic understandings of the topic you are studying. An example of a generalization for this theme is: "Animals grow and change for survival." Generalizations should be written as a conclusion or final thought that can be proved or disproved with support from information you found while researching the topic. Using generalizations to explain a topic or idea can help you to get the main points across in a quick and easy manner. Once you get the main idea across, details can be added that provide support to your ideas.

Directions

Write at least five generalizations about the theme of Animals.

1. _____

_____

2. _____

_____

3. _____

_____

4. _____

_____

5. _____

_____

Thinking Quests

• In what ways do animals impact the way we live? At home? At school? At work? At play? In our state? In our country? In our continent? In the world? In what ways are these impacts the same? In what ways are these impacts different?

• How has your understanding of animals changed throughout these activities? Identify at least three ideas or questions that need to be considered in the future.

Flowering Plants

Flower Find

Have you ever gone to look for something and not been able to find it? Then, when you go back to look for it again, it was right in front of you? Everyone experiences times when they overlook objects. You may have walked past a flower or bush dozens of times and never noticed it, but when you are studying flowering plants, your attention is drawn to this plant. A word find is a great game that helps train our eyes to look for things that are around us. It encourages us to look for details.

Directions

Use the words listed in the box to complete the word find. Words are placed vertically, horizontally, backward, or on the diagonal. Letters can be used more than once, and the words may overlap. Circle the letters that form words. You will not use every letter.

I	A	T	L	I	L	Y	O	E	I	H	E	V	A	N
N	X	V	I	O	L	E	T	O	R	T	S	Q	U	W
D	W	B	L	S	V	A	I	L	O	N	G	A	M	B
I	K	D	Y	H	O	F	Y	J	S	A	E	N	H	C
A	R	F	O	R	G	E	T	M	E	N	O	T	L	M
N	E	Z	F	G	F	V	Z	R	N	Y	C	O	A	W
P	W	D	T	G	W	S	O	Y	P	Z	V	I	X	N
A	O	O	H	C	R	O	C	P	D	E	L	M	O	O
I	L	R	E	K	P	A	O	V	R	L	E	G	R	I
N	F	N	V	P	L	P	T	D	I	O	A	E	C	T
T	N	E	A	I	C	U	I	W	L	R	T	S	H	A
B	U	D	L	R	S	G	T	U	D	U	K	M	I	N
R	S	L	L	I	T	E	U	P	L	J	Q	U	D	R
U	D	O	E	S	E	Y	A	I	N	U	T	E	P	A
S	L	G	Y	W	D	N	P	L	P	O	M	R	X	C
H	N	A	S	U	S	D	E	Y	E	K	C	A	L	B

Word Box:

Lily of the Valley
Black Eyed Susan
Carnation
Sunflower
Violet
Petunia
Lilac
Snap Dragon
Dogwood
Rose
Magnolia
Lily
Indian Paintbrush
Sweet William
Poppy
Iris
Forget Me Not
Orchid
Tulip
Clover
Goldenrod

Thinking Quest

- Create a list of 20 flowering plants and make your own word find. Your word find can have a theme, such as "Wild Flowers" or "Fruits and Vegetables." Make a copy of this and use it as an answer key. Then, have your friends try to find the plant names within your game.

WORD FIND
Created by _____

A Flower's Parts

What makes plants living things? All plants are able to move, respire, have structure, grow, reproduce, and make their own food. They have been on Earth for millions of years. Plantlike fossils first appeared in rocks of the Silurian period (430 to 408 million years ago). Although researchers are still studying the origins of flowering plants, it is believed they have been around for 130 million years.

Directions

When studying flowering plants, it is important to be able to identify and know the function of the various parts. Using the diagram below and the word bank, identify the parts. Make a chart that describes the purpose of each part and discusses how these parts work together to make the flower function.

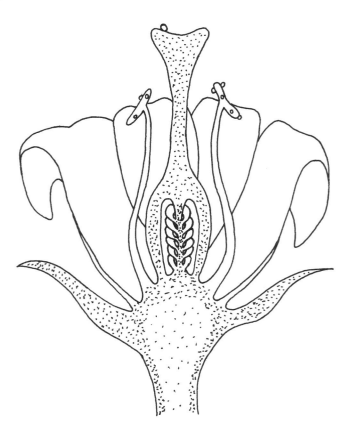

stigma

peduncle

receptacle

sepal

anther

stamen

perianth

filament

ovary

developing seed

style

petal

Thinking Quests

- Consider what would happen if the plant did not have petals. Would the plant survive if it did not have a stigma? What accommodations would have to be made for the flowering plant to survive if it were missing certain parts? Make a chart that lists the parts of the flower and discuss what would happen if the plant were missing each specific part and the accommodations that would need to be made for the plant's survival.

- Research to see if there are any plants that do not have all of these parts and, if so, the changes they had to make in order to survive. Do insects or the environment play a role in the plant's life cycle?

Flowering Plant Uses

The rosy periwinkle plant is a source of chemical compounds that can be used to treat diseases such as cancer. Plant species are often used as ingredients in medicines. In fact, 40 different plant species make up more than 25% of the prescription drugs sold in the United States. We depend on plants for our health, nutrition, and beauty.

Directions

Make a list of at least 10 people whose jobs involve the use of flowering plants. The most obvious is a florist, but there are also many people who use plants in unique or unexpected ways, such as a perfume designer. Once your list is complete, provide two or three examples of how each person uses flowering plants in his or her job.

1. _____

2. _____

3. _____

4. _____

5. _____

6. _____

7. _____

8. _____

9. _____

10. _____

Thinking Quests

- Select two of the jobs listed above and research the work they do with flowering plants. What knowledge do people in these positions need to know about plants? What is their experience and educational background?

- The scientific community has started altering the genes of various plants to make them stronger. This is called *genetic engineering*. Discuss three benefits of using genetically altered plants in the jobs listed above. Identify three ways that genetically altered plants could damage those same jobs.

Watch Them Grow

All living things grow and develop at different rates. Think about your friends. As you have been growing up, you may have noticed that not everyone lost their baby teeth at the same time and not everyone was able to ride a bicycle without training wheels at the same time. These are called *developmental differences*. By now, your friends have probably all lost their baby teeth and are all able to ride a bicycle, but the differences in time that it took to do these things varied from one person to another. These same developmental differences can be seen when looking at both plants and animals of the same species and across species.

Directions

Get a variety of seeds/bulbs (lima beans, tulip bulbs, marigold seeds, onions, etc.). Plant three of each seed according to their specific directions and graph the growth of both the individual seeds and the different species. Measure the growth of each plant every day and note any changes you notice happening (appearance of leaves, flowers, fruit, etc.). At the end of every week, write two to three sentences about your findings for the week in a plant journal. After several weeks, compare and contrast the development of each species and the development across species. Share your findings with a friend. Was there one plant species that did better than another? Why do you think this happened? Explain.

Thinking Quest

- Consider the growth of the plant and the size of the original seed. Do you notice any similarities? Do the smaller seeds grow quicker? What could you do to make plants grow faster? Do certain fertilizers help? Does more water or more sunlight help in the growth and development of plants? Conduct several experiments to see if you can find any ways to improve plant growth. When you are increasing plant development, is the plant just as strong? Does it produce just as many leaves, flowers, or seeds? How would you judge the quality of the quick-growing plant compared to the original development time? Should farmers use quick growing methods? Why or why not?

Arrangement and Storage

Libraries organize their books in certain orders or systems. Botanists, people who study plants, organize their plants in systems, too. Often times, plants will be stored in a herbarium. Plants in a herbarium are normally called *specimens* because they represent a sample of what the plant is like. Specimens may be pressed flat and dried in the compartments of herbarium cabinets, preserved in jars filled with special fluid, or air dried and stored in boxes. If taken care of properly, specimens may last over 100 years and help to keep a record of the flora and fauna of a certain time and place, the collections of certain botanists, or even migration patterns. Therefore, it is important to collect and store plants in a way that will make them last.

Materials

- Pruning sheers
- Newspaper
- Telephone book
- Heavy books
- Three-ring binder
- Clear, plastic page sleeves

Directions

When collecting and preserving flowering plants, you only need to select one flower on the plant for your collection. Look carefully at the flowers and select one. While the flower is still fresh, put it between two sheets of newspaper. Place the newspaper between the pages of an old telephone book. Then, put heavy books on top of the telephone book (this pressure helps to remove moisture from the plant and allows the flower to stay flat). Each day, change the newspaper, place it between two clean pages of the telephone book, and then reapply the heavy books. After 7–10 days, the flowering plant you selected should be dry. There are a variety of ways you can preserve your flower. You can mount it in a three-ring binder between plastic slip covers and create a scrap book, or you can have it framed.

Thinking Quest

- Create labels for the plants you have collected and preserved. Labels for plants in herbariums contain the following information: a title (the name of the herbarium where the collection is kept) and the name of the special collection or the individual plant. Some collections contain maps of the collecting area and identify from where the specific sample came. Because botanists are interested in the name of each plant and where it came from, they also include the following information in their collections: the scientific name of the plant, the name of the person who named the plant, the common name of the plant, the specific location where the plant was found, and descriptions of the plant's habitat (if it grows in the sun or shade; woods, marsh, field, water; the type of soil it grows in).

National Symbols

When we think of birds that represent peace, we may think of a dove. This bird is an example of a symbol— an abstract idea expressed by an object that can be seen and touched. All countries and cultures have symbols that represent ideas specific to their beliefs. You may see these symbols on flags, money, or even hear about them in national anthems. For example, Canada's flag has a maple leaf, and Mexico's flag has an eagle holding a snake. Every state in the United States has its own tree, flower, and bird to represent its heritage.

Directions

Write the name of the flower, tree, and bird for each state listed below. Identify if the state flags include any symbols specific to their heritage. If so, how are these symbols meaningful to the people of that state? A Web site that may be useful is The Garden Helper (http://www.thegardenhelper.com/state-flowers.html), which lists official state flowers, trees, and birds for each state.

	Flower	Tree	Bird
1. Maryland	_____	_____	_____
Flag symbols:	_____		
2. Texas	_____	_____	_____
Flag symbols:	_____		
3. Florida	_____	_____	_____
Flag symbols:	_____		
4. Louisiana	_____	_____	_____
Flag symbols:	_____		
5. Tennessee	_____	_____	_____
Flag symbols:	_____		

6. Hawaii   _____   _____   _____

   Flag symbols: _____

7. Nebraska   _____   _____   _____

   Flag symbols: _____

8. Maine   _____   _____   _____

   Flag symbols: _____

9. California   _____   _____   _____

   Flag symbols: _____

10. Minnesota   _____   _____   _____

   Flag symbols: _____

Thinking Quests

- Look over a list of all of the names of state flowers. Compile a list of states that selected the same flower as their state flower. What flowers were the most popular? Did you notice any patterns of where these flowers occurred? Use the map in the Appendix to make a visual representation of your findings. For example, a key or legend may show that you decided to color all of the states that had the sunflower as their state flower the same color. Make a similar map for the trees and/or birds.

- Select a minimum of 10 different countries from around the world. For each country, draw a picture of its flag and share the symbolism represented in its design.

- Identify symbols that represent you as a person. Make your own flag and identify a bird, flower, and tree that represent ideas or beliefs about you and your family. Write a description of why you selected these items.

Detective Work

Railroad tracks, back alleys, country roads, waterfronts, porches, cracks in the sidewalk, vacant lots, and gardens. What do all these have in common? You can find plants in and around each of these locations. In areas where there are people or shipments coming from many different locations, you will find unusual plants. These plants are typically brought in accidentally from other geographical areas.

Materials

- Graph paper
- Yardstick or tape measurer

- Pencil
- Ruler

Directions

Look around your neighborhood or school and identify at least 10 flowering plants. Some you may already know by sight, others you may need to identify by looking at a guidebook about plants. Make a bird's-eye-view map of the area you visited and identify the location of the plants. Make the map to scale. To do this, you will need to measure the area (length x width) you visited with a yardstick or tape measurer. When determining the scale you will use for your map, you will need to convert the feet to inches. For example, 1 inch on your paper = 1 yard (3 feet) in real life. Put your scale in the key or legend of your map. Then, label and color the plants you identified. Make sure the plants are also drawn to scale.

Thinking Quests

- Dry and press the plants you identified in your map. Make a catalog of the plants growing around your neighborhood, around your school, or at a local park.

- Claude Monet was known for drawing and painting in his garden. Draw or paint the various flowering plants identified above. How many different shades of green do you notice among the plants? Why do you think they are the same? Why do you think they are different?

- Look carefully at the plants you identified above. Are all of these plants indigenous to this region—are they part of the area's heritage? Were some of them brought to this area or planted here? How do you think they got here? What is the function of each plant? Are they helpful, harmful, or both? Explain. Share your findings in a chart.

What is This?

Scientists and researchers have identified over a half million different plant species. Every year, new plant species are found around the world, especially in the tropics. It is believed that there may be another half million species not yet discovered. Even though plants have a classification system similar to that used by animals, the observable differences are not as striking among plants. Many plants have subtle differences that are based on their chemical make-up, which helps protect them against fungi, animals, and other plants. Because plants can look similar, chemical analysis often has to be done to determine if a new plant species has been found.

Directions

When walking through an unknown area, you may come across a new plant. Should you touch it? Is it a plant you can eat? Identify the characteristics that make these two plants different from their surroundings:

- Poison Ivy
- Poison Sumac
- Poison Oak

How can we identify these plants in their natural environment? What plants look similar but do not cause harm?

Thinking Quests

- Present your findings on these two plants to a local group or organization. Share your findings using pictures, charts, and graphs. Write a report on the types of questions you were asked. Then, make a brochure that addresses these types of questions and provides the answers.

- There is often discussion about how poison ivy should be sprayed and killed in order to help keep people safe from possible infection. Debate this topic and find the positive points for why poisonous plants should be allowed to grow and the counterargument for why these plants should be removed from their natural environment. Make a poster that summarizes the points you identified and share it with your peers.

Exploring Ecosystems

Plants (both land and shallow marine) are responsible for changing the sun's energy, water, and carbon dioxide into food, fiber, coal, oil, wood, and other types of stored energy. Survival would be difficult, if not impossible, without plant life. Maintaining the balance plants need is a difficult task, and mini environments called *ecosystems* or *biospheres* can be created within your classroom. Biospheres are totally enclosed ecosystems that are self-contained and self-sustaining. This means they use the plant and animal resources available within their environment without overpopulating or contaminating their environment. This is able to occur because the plants and animals work together to keep the oxygen and carbon dioxide amounts in equal balance.

Materials

- 2 two-liter soft drink bottles (clear)
- soil
- small plants with roots

Directions

1. Cut the soft drink bottle about 4 inches from the base.
2. Add soil to the base and then arrange the small plant(s) in the soil. Pack the soil around the plants, leaving approximately 3/4 inch of space between the soil and the edge of the base.
3. Water the plant, making sure the soil is moist.
4. Cut the other soft drink bottle approximately 8 inches from the bottom. This portion of the bottle will be the top of your biosphere. The distance you cut the bottle can range; however, it is important to make sure that you have enough extra room to fit this portion over your plants.
5. Turn the newly cut portion of the bottle upside down and place it over (covering) the base, which is holding the plants. This fit should be tight, as this seal is important in the functioning of your biosphere. If you cannot get the bottles to fit together, it may be helpful to cut a small slit in the top of the biosphere.
6. Place your biosphere in a location where it gets regular amounts of sunlight.

Thinking Quests

- Keep a journal of the changes you notice in your biosphere. What roles do sunlight and water play in the success of a biosphere? What happens to the water you originally put in the biosphere? Draw a picture that describes what happens to the water, oxygen, and carbon dioxide within a biosphere. Label the stages that occur. Identify other locations where similar cycles occur.

- Construct an aquatic biosphere with algae, brine shrimp, snails, aquatic insects, or even sea monkeys. The following Web site about homemade biospheres may be useful in constructing your own: http://www.frii.com/~dboll/ecospher.htm. What are the additional needs of a biosphere containing each of these? How can the needs be balanced? What role does algae play in this process? How are water, oxygen, and carbon dioxide exchanged within this environment?

Flowering Plants
Generalizations

If you had 5 minutes to tell someone about flowering plants, what would you say? This is a difficult task, even for people who study plants for a living. When thinking about the theme of Flowering Plants, there are often important ideas we can take away that will help us to think about and remember how plants function. These important ideas are called *generalizations*. Generalizations are based on factual information or basic understandings of the topic you are studying. An example of a generalization for this theme is: "Flowering plants grow and change for survival." Generalizations should be written as a conclusion or final thought that can be proved or disproved with support from information you found while researching the topic. Using generalizations to explain a topic or idea can help you to get the main points across in a quick and easy manner. Once you get the main idea across, details can be added that provide support to your ideas.

Directions

Write at least five generalizations about the theme of Flowering Plants.

1. _____

_____

2. _____

_____

3. _____

_____

4. _____

_____

5. _____

_____

Thinking Quests

- In what ways do flowering plants impact the way we live? At home? At school? At work? At play? In our state? In our country? In our continent? In the world? In what ways are these impacts the same? In what ways are these impacts different?

- How has your understanding of flowering plants changed throughout these activities? Identify at least three ideas or questions that need to be considered in the future.

Bugs

Examine a Bug

It is estimated that there are more than 50 million bugs that live on Earth, but only about 10 million have been formally described and named by scientists. In fact, bugs are the most dominant life form on the planet. They mainly eat plants, but also help in the breakdown, or decomposition, of plant and animal material. In addition, bugs are a source of food for many other animals. Bugs live in most environments, including deserts and Antarctica. There are approximately 200 fully aquatic bugs, but these are not as common. Because there are so many different types of bugs and their jobs vary depending on their environment, there are a few characteristics that all bugs have in common.

Directions

When studying bugs, it is important to be able to identify and know the function of each bug's various parts. The size, form, and behavior of these parts may be different depending on the type of bug you find. Using the diagram on the next page and the word bank below, identify the parts. Make a chart that describes the purpose of each part and discusses how these parts work together to make a bug function. The "Introduction to Insect Anatomy" at the Web site Earthlife.net (http://www.earthlife.net/insects/anatomy.html) gives an overview of the basic parts that make up a bug's body.

exoskeleton	head	thorax	abdomen
legs	spiracles	mandible	antennae
clypeus	labrum	scape	compound eyes
maxillae	coxa	trochanter	femur
tarsus	tibia	claws	

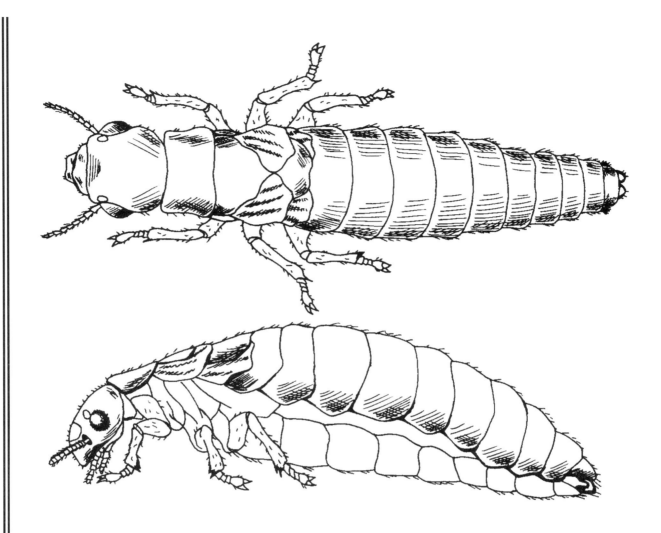

Thinking Quests

- Bugs are part of the phylum called *arthropoda*. All arthropods have segmented bodies, segmented legs, and an exoskeleton. Arthropoda are divided into four classes: insecta (insects), arachnida (spiders, mites, ticks), diplopoda (millipedes), and chilopoda (centipedes). Draw a picture of the four different classes of arthropods and identify their features. Make a chart that lists the parts of the bugs and identify which of the four classes of arthropoda have these characteristics. Why did researchers divide the arthropoda into these four classes? Select three additional bugs, draw a picture of them, label their parts, and identify the kingdom, phylum, and class. Explain why you put each bug in its category.

- Make a model of a bug. Use materials you find around your house, at school, or both, for example, shoe boxes, aluminum cans, baby food jars, construction paper, pipe cleaners, cotton balls, pieces of fabric, dried leaves, tissue paper, paint, and glue. Make the body parts for your bug and put them all together. Share your creation.

Let's Fly

All bugs in the class insecta have three pairs of legs, three body sections, either one or two pairs of wings, and one pair of antennae. From looking at fossil records, some scientists believe that insects are the only animal on land, besides birds and bats that evolved the ability to fly. In fact, it is believed that insects flew before the evolution of the insect-hunting bat. Insects are able to fly because of their small body size and their striated muscle development. Striated muscles allow rapid, strong contractions of muscle groups, similar to those muscles used by hummingbirds in flight. Flight is a characteristic that makes insects different from other classes of bugs.

Directions

Put the following bugs in alphabetical order.

honeybee   ant   cockroach   termite   mealybug

dragonfly   tick   mite   spider   scorpion   springtail

silverfish   firebrat   mayfly   damselfly   stonefly   grasshopper

cricket   katydid   mandit   walking stick   earwig   psocid

booklice   louse   thrip   leafhopper   scale   aphid

lacewing   antlion   boll weevil   pecan weevil   millipede

white grub   ladybird beetle   scorpionfly   true fly

mosquito   gnat   midge   carpenter bee   yellow jacket

hornet   cicada killer   mud dauber   caddisflies   moth

butterfly   clothes moth   cut worm   flea   centipede

Then, make a chart like the one below for the four classes of arthropoda: insecta, arachnida, diplopoda, and chilopoda. Place a check mark in the appropriate box to indicate the class to which each bug belongs.

Bug Names	Insecta	Arachnida	Diplopoda	Chilopoda

Thinking Quests

- Research at least two bugs from each class. What are the characteristics of this bug? Identify the characteristics for it being in the kingdom anamalia, the phylum arthropoda, and the specific class. Where does this animal live (environment, climate)? How does this animal breathe (respire)? What type of support system does this animal have (skeleton, cartilage)? How does this animal react to other stimuli (animals, the environment)? How does it eat and digest food? How does it move? How does it protect itself? How does it reproduce? How does it care for its young? Is it warm- or cold-blooded?

- Using the research you gathered about the bugs in the four classes, discuss in what ways bugs from the same class are similar and how they are they different. What things would have to change on one bug to make it a member of another class? For example, what would a spider look like if it became a millipede? Draw a picture of this new bug and explain how it would function and behave.

Find the Right Letters

Many bugs are similar in how they look, but are different in how they move, what they eat, or even how they reproduce. For example, there are many different types of spiders, some are venomous and others are not. The Brown Recluse Spider has a bite that may make you sick. It is also known as the Fiddleback Spider because it has a violin pattern near its head. Additional characteristics of this spider include legs with fine hairs, rather than thick spines. The Brown Recluse has six eyes (arranged in pairs) with one pair pointing toward the front and the other two pairs on the sides of the thorax, whereas most spiders in the U.S. have eight eyes in two rows of four. Being able to identify the Brown Recluse Spider requires a careful eye.

Directions

Look carefully at the bug names below and fill in the missing letters. Use each letter once.

1. B U __ __ E R __ __ Y

2. M O __ Q __ I __ O

3. __ R A S __ H O __ P E __

4. __ L E __

5. M O __ __

6. W A __ __

7. C R I __ __ E __

8. __ A D __ B U __

K	C	R	P	T	U	T	A	T	S	H	F
T	S	L	S	G	F	P	T	L	Y	G	

55

Thinking Quests

- Select three bugs about which you want to find more information. For each bug, make a list of its characteristics. Include the bug's name, the names of its body parts, stages in its life cycle, information about its habitat, what it eats, and so forth. Reference books and Web sites may be helpful in locating insect related words. For example, try The Butterfly WebSite (http://butterflywebsite.com) for general information about butterflies. Use the words you find to create your own Missing Letter Puzzle. Make a key to the puzzle and let your friends try it.

- Select one of the bugs from above and write a story about what a day would be like as this animal. What would it look like where you sleep? What would wake you up? What would you eat? Would you work? Would you have to gather pollen? Would you chew on timber or trees? Do you like the work you do? Do you get along with other bugs of your same kind? What is your favorite thing to do during the day? What is your least favorite thing to do during the day? Include characteristics of that bug in your description.

Helpful or Harmful?

The body parts of bugs have specific functions and roles. For example, termites normally have huge mouthparts, or mandibles, which can be used to defend their colony from the invasion of ants. The mandibles also carry food to colony members. When bugs eat or migrate from one location to another, they may transmit diseases such as bacteria, fungi, or viruses. The mosquito has been known to carry a microbe that causes malaria. Bugs, however, are not always harmful. In fact, less than 1% of bugs are pests, and only a few hundred of these are thought of as a problem. Because bugs are also a major source of food, many birds and some animals would not survive without them. In addition, bugs are helpful to us for they produce silk, honey, wax, and many other products.

Directions

Match the bugs in the box below with the different ways they may be harmful. Some bugs may be used more than once. Then, using these same bugs, make your own list of how they are helpful.

- Build webs to capture prey

- Pests on animals and humans

- Chew on books and household items

- Predators

- Eat plants

- Structural pests

- Helpful?

spider	caterpillar	silverfish	tick	aphid	termite
beetle	louse	cockroach	booklouse	mayfly	
dragonfly	mandit	earwig	thrip	Stonefly	
grasshopper	mosquito	scorpion fly	flea	true bug	

Thinking Quests

- Sometimes, bugs are considered pests by farmers because they damage crops, which results in a loss of income. But, at the same time, bugs help keep our environment in balance. What do we consider when deciding if an insect is helpful or harmful? Can you think of some cultures where a bug would be seen as helpful and other cultures in which it would be seen as harmful? Why do they have this different opinion? Why is it important to gain knowledge about how bugs behave, their natural enemies, and how their bodies work?

- Bugs are all around us. They help pollinate flowering plants, they eat plants, and they help to decompose plant and animal matter. When certain species of bugs die off because of pesticide use, there is a change in the natural habitat and other life forms are affected. This change is called an *ecological transformation*. For example, if grasshoppers were to die off because of pesticide use, what would happen to the birds that eat grasshoppers? Would they die, too? Consider this balance and decide if pesticides should be used to protect our plant life. Explain your answer.

Growing Up

Have you ever noticed your shoes getting too tight around the toes or your jeans getting a bit too short? Bugs also change sizes as they mature—growing from a small larva to an adult. They may even change form, such as the caterpillar changing into a butterfly. This change in physical form is called *metamorphosis*. Not all bugs change like the butterfly. However, all bugs have a life cycle composed of four separate stages through which they pass: egg, larva or nymph, pupa, and adult. After the larva comes out of the egg, over time it grows bigger. The larva molts or sheds its outer skin (exoskeleton) between each stage. All growth for a bug occurs during the larval stage; but, because insects are cold-blooded, the rate at which they grow and develop depends on the temperature of their environment.

Directions

Observe the development of a butterfly from an egg, to a caterpillar, to a chrysalis, to a monarch. Monarch kits are available at many educational supply stores and may be purchased on the Internet through Live Monarch (http://www.livemonarch.com). Keep a journal of your observations and draw a picture of the butterfly's development every day for approximately 1 month. What transitions do you notice? Make a diagram of the development of the monarch and share your findings with friends. Identify the factors that may influence a monarch's development.

Thinking Quests

- Monarch butterflies follow migration patterns and move from one place to another depending on the climate and season. Using the map in the Appendix, draw the progression of the monarch's migration pattern. How far does the monarch normally fly? What does the monarch have to do to prepare for the journey? How does the monarch protect itself? What types of things can hurt or kill a monarch (pests, pesticides, pollution, loss of habitat, etc.)? Can monarchs cause damage to plants and trees?

- Have you ever noticed that mosquitoes bite the most right around sundown? This is about the same time lightning bugs come out. In fact, locust eggs hatch only when environmental conditions are favorable for success. But, if the bugs are still just eggs, how do they know when to hatch? Bugs of all types seem to know when to prepare for winter, when it is best to hatch, and when there is a change in the time of day.

How do they know? If bugs cannot read calendars or tell time with clocks, then how are they able to keep track of these seasonal changes? Are these abilities part of the bug's genetic make-up? Are they just born able to do these things? Or, do they pick up on cues from their environment using their senses? Select one bug and research these questions.

Open Your Eyes

Ecologists are people who study the interactions between organisms and the environment. For an insect, the environment may include physical and biological factors. Physical factors may include the temperature, wind, humidity, available sunlight, physical location, and altitude. Biological factors may depend on predators and the number of other species competing for natural resources such as food, water, and shelter. In order to understand the life cycle of a bug, it is necessary to look at how all these factors impact its daily life. These day-to-day interactions the bug has with the environment relate to its success, activity level, and diversity. For example, if a spider lives in a location where its natural food source, flying insects, is in short supply, it might starve. In taking these factors into consideration, we can better understand how to deal with the bug if pest management is necessary.

Directions

Follow two different bugs for 20 minutes each. While following the bugs, observe their interactions with the environment by watching them carefully and closely. It may be helpful to use a magnifying glass. Look specifically for signs of physical and biological factors that may impact these bugs. While you are observing, ask yourself:

- What am I noticing?

- Did I think this would occur?

- Am I surprised at what I am seeing?

- What is happening that I did not anticipate?

- Would this same thing happen during the night?

- Would it happen during a different season?

- Can I come to some conclusions after this observation?

Thinking Quests

- Look over the notes you made about the two different bugs. What physical factors were similar between the two bugs? Did they respond in the same way to the challenges? Why or why not? What physical factors were different? How did this change the way the bugs responded? Did you notice any biological factors? What were these? Identify several physical and environmental factors that you did not observe. How do you think these bugs would have responded to these changes? Would they have responded in the same way? Explain.

- Select two bugs of the same type you observed before. Follow the procedures above. Then, compare your findings to your previously collected notes. Were the characteristics the same? Were there any differences? Why is it better to observe a group of several different bugs of the same species than to observe just one bug? If you were studying a group of bugs that were considered pests, how might studying the group versus the individual change your findings?

Working Together

In forests, bugs have many functions. They may be invaders, consumers, or scavengers. Invaders, such as termites and bark beetles, eat dead and dying trees and plants. In doing this, these bugs help to start the decomposition process, the breaking down of matter to create soil. Consumers, such as daddy long legs, centipedes, and ants, eat other organisms and their remains. Scavengers, like the wood roach, eat dead and decaying plant or animal matter; they may live in the fallen logs and on the forest floor. Even though bugs have different roles and responsibilities, they need one another in order to live. This reliance upon others in the forest is part of the forest's ecosystem.

Materials

• Magnifying glass

Directions

Visit a park or forest and examine logs or fallen leaves and twigs. Be careful not to disturb or collect organisms during your observation, as this may disturb the ecosystem on which they depend. Identify the different decomposers, consumers, and scavengers you find. Draw a picture of the bugs in their natural environment and identify how they help each other. Are there organisms other than bugs that help the bugs live? How do all of these things work together to make a healthy ecosystem?

Thinking Quests

• Using the knowledge you have gained in the study of bugs, compare and contrast some bug characteristics to those of mammals and plants. How are bugs similar to mammals and plants? How are they different? Do mammals and plants work as decomposers, consumers, and scavengers? Explain.

• Draw five pictures that show what life is like on the log, branch, or leaf you observed above. Make the first picture of the log showing what the item looked like if you were just looking at it, without a magnifying glass. Then, draw a picture of what it looks like using the magnifying glass and another using the view of a microscope. Now, draw the item as if you were standing 5 steps away and then 20 steps away. As you draw these pictures, your paper should be filled with the item; however, the amount of detail you show will increase or decrease, depending on how close to or far away from the log you are. How are these pictures showing different ways to view an ecosystem?

Collecting and Preserving

In looking at how bugs live in our world, we can get a better understanding of how our world works. Bugs live everywhere. You can find them in and around boards and rocks, compost piles, the ground, manure, animals and plants, animal nests or burrows, stream or pond water, the air, near lights, and in swimming pools. You can make a collection of bugs to help you learn their names and the specific characteristics of each species.

Materials

- Insect pins
- Container for collecting bugs
- Butterfly net
- Tissue paper or paper towels
- Fingernail polish remover
- Mounting board

Directions

Search the above locations and collect at least 10 different samples of bugs. Put each bug in a jar that has a piece of tissue paper for it to crawl on. Bugs are best preserved in a jar that contains a paper towel with a small amount of fingernail polish remover or by simply placing a jar with the bug inside it in the freezer. Once the bug is preserved, use insect pins to tack the bug's right side to a mount. By pinning just the right side, the left side will remain complete so you can study the bug's characteristics. Tack the bug to the mounting board and place a label below the pin. By including a label below the bug, it becomes a specimen. Labels should include the state (in all caps), county, location, and date of collection. The day and year should be written in Arabic numerals, and the month should be written in Roman numerals. Also include the name of the person who collected the specimen and any other special information.

Thinking Quests

- In *Joyful Noise*, Paul Fleischman wrote poems from the perspective of bugs. His poems talk about the activities and characteristics of many different types of bugs. Write your own riddles or poems about the bugs you collected above. Make your own book to hold your writings. Be creative in your design.

- Gary Larson, the creator of *The Far Side*, used bugs (and other animals) in his cartoons. He often made jokes about the fears we may have about bugs or how they are considered pests. For example, most people have a fear of finding a bug in their shoe, especially a scorpion. In one cartoon, two scorpions are talking to one another on the edge of a shoe, and, in the background, you see a person's feet lying on the floor as if the person fell over. One scorpion, with his claws and stinger in the air, says to the other, "There I was! Asleep in this little cave here, when suddenly I was attacked by this hideous thing with five heads." In creating his humor, Larson often took the perspective of the bug. Make at least four different cartoons around bugs and bug humor.

It Can't Be!

Franz Kafka's book *The Metamorphosis* tells the story of a young man who wakes up one morning as a cockroach. As you can imagine, this change would significantly impact what could and could not be done during a normal day. When authors write stories, they often have different types of messages or themes running through them. Kafka's book can be read straight as a story about a man who turns into a bug, or you can look at the underlying themes, such as how the character feels isolated, alone, and without friends. This is because, when we think of bugs, we tend to think of them as being alone. How often do you see bugs in groups? If you see just one, do you ever wonder where the others are?

Directions

Use the prompt below to write a story about how your day would change if you woke up as a bug. Tell about where you go, funny things that happen, and how it feels to be a bug. Keep in mind the physical and behavioral characteristics of your bug, as well as how people tend to react when they see a bug of this kind. You might begin like this:

> Pretend that early one morning, as you slowly opened your eyes to greet the bright morning sun, you felt very different, very unusual, very much . . . well, let's say you just "were not yourself."
>
> You gently pushed back the covers on the bed, and ever so slowly you began to pull your arm out from under the blanket. But, wait, instead of pulling out one arm and then another, you pulled out one, another, another, and yes, another until you had six, yes, *six* arms all resting on your blanket.
>
> You sprang from your bed and flew to the mirror over your dresser.
>
> "It can't be!" you said right out loud.
>
> But, it was true. You had become a bug.
>
> In the middle of the night, something very strange had occurred in your bedroom.

Thinking Quests

• Using the story you wrote above, create a play about your life as a bug. Write the script, design the set, and draw a picture of your costume(s). Are there any songs you could sing? Could you change the words of songs you know to make them fit your play? Share your ideas with friends and stage the play for an audience.

- Different countries and cultures have similar ways of understanding the world, but take a variety of perspectives to explain why it works the way it does. In the book *Why Mosquitoes Buzz in People's Ears: A West African Tale*, retold by Verna Aardema, readers come to an understanding of mosquito behavior. Create your own story to explain a bug's activities, behaviors, or both.

Bug Generalizations

I f you had 5 minutes to tell someone about bugs, what would you say? This is a difficult task, even for people who study bugs for a living. When thinking about the theme of Bugs, there are often important ideas we can take away that will help us to think about and remember how bugs function. These important ideas are called *generalizations*. Generalizations are based on factual information or basic understandings of the topic you are studying. An example of a generalization for this theme is: "Bugs grow and change for survival." Generalizations should be written as a conclusion or final thought that can be proved or disproved with support from information you found while researching the topic. Using generalizations to explain a topic or idea can help you to get the main points across in a quick and easy manner. Once you get the main idea across, details can be added that provide support to your ideas.

Directions

Write at least five generalizations about the theme of Bugs.

1. _____

_____

2. _____

_____

3. _____

_____

4. _____

_____

5. _____

_____

Thinking Quests

- In what ways do bugs impact the way we live? At home? At school? At work? At play? In our state? In our country? In our continent? In the world? Our environment? In what ways are these impacts the same? In what ways are these impacts different?

- How has your understanding of bugs changed throughout these activities? Identify at least three ideas or questions that need to be considered in the future.

Sports and Outdoor Activities

Let's Pretend

Have you ever watched someone get worked up about how a team performs or a referee's call? Have you seen people not respond at all to that same situation? How we react to our environment and the things that go on around us depends on our level of emotional excitement, which fluctuates from low (very sleepy), to medium (ability to perform your best), to high (causing you to be disorganized or even paralyzed with fear). Psychologists believe that our level of emotional excitement is linked to how efficient we are in our day-to-day actions.

Directions

Pantomime with a friend. Pretend you are a fan watching your favorite sports event. Change your levels of emotional excitement from low, to medium, to high. Show your friend how you would react when your team gains points, when a member of your team misses an important play, when the other team gains points, when you see a player make a strong play, and when your team wins the game. How does your level of emotional excitement impact your reactions?

Thinking Quests

• Make a flip book illustrating the progression of one of your emotions during the event you are watching. Try to show your emotions through dark lines, facial expressions, or even adding color. Share this with your friends. What level of emotional excitement is your character expressing? Why?

• Pantomime three different sporting events with a friend. How did your reactions change from one event to the other? For example, should you show the same enthusiasm when watching a tennis match or golf tournament that you would show when watching a professional wrestling match? Explain. Are there any social expectations for how you should behave at these events? What are these unspoken rules for the events you pantomimed? Why are these expectations important?

This Looks Fishy

Careful distinctions have to be made by players in all sports and outdoor activities. Even when attempting to catch fish, one has to have an eye on the details: How tight should the line be? What is the difference between a fish nibbling on your line and accidentally hooking sea weed? When is the best time to try to catch a fish? The morning? The afternoon? The evening? Before a rainstorm? What type of bait should be used? Worms? Flies? Crawfish? Minnows? If you use fake bait, should it be colored? What will lure the fish to your bait? Taking into consideration all of these factors, fishing can be much more technical than it might appear. For this reason, it is important for fishermen to pay close attention to details.

Directions

The following words are all related to the sport of fishing. However, they have been scrambled up. Look for clues that may help you to unscramble these words.

1. odr   _____

2. eelr   _____

3. stca   _____

4. rule   _____

5. abit   _____

6. erbbbo   _____

7. okoh   _____

8. mowr   _____

9. sihf   _____

10. yfl   _____

Thinking Quests

- Write your own list of at least 10 scrambled words about either sports or outdoor activities. Make an answer key for yourself and then let a friend try to figure out your list.

- Using your unscrambled words, illustrate the game or sporting event and include each of the words in your drawing. For example, if your topic were ice skating, you would want to draw and label the rink, ice skates, flowers, medals, blades, and so forth.

- Select a sport or outdoor activity that you can use for a theme on a scavenger hunt. Create a list of at least 15 different items (equipment, tools, supplies) that are used during this activity. Exchange lists with a friend and then search for the items on your list. After you find the items, identify how each are used and why they are useful.

Special Equipment

Athletes use equipment during both practice and competitions. Sporting equipment or gear is used for several reasons. The two main reasons athletes use equipment that is specifically designed for their sport are to help them participate in a stronger manner and to protect themselves from injury. All sports use specific equipment. For example, bicyclists wear helmets to protect their skulls in case they get into an accident. Some sports equipment is specifically designed to help athletes perform at a better level. For example, some bicycle helmets have ventilation to keep the cyclist cool and are aerodynamically shaped to decrease wind resistance.

Directions

Match the equipment with the sport. Write the number of each piece of equipment on the line next to the game or sport in which it is used.

1.	goggles	_____	golf
2.	hurdles	_____	hopscotch
3.	putter	_____	swimming
4.	net	_____	gymnastics
5.	paddle	_____	soccer
6.	pebbles	_____	track
7.	beam	_____	volleyball
8.	mallet	_____	canoeing
9.	goal	_____	croquet

Thinking Quests

* Select a sport or game and generate a list of the equipment that is needed to play it. Search the Internet for stores that sell that equipment. Identify if the equipment is designed for safety or for enhanced performance. Explain how the design of the equipment helps athletes. Then, design your own version of the equipment and create an advertising campaign to promote its benefits.

- Make a list of as many different sports and games you can think of in 10 minutes. Circle at least five that you find fun, original, or interesting and use them to make your own book. Draw the equipment and uniforms needed to play and write the rules. You may even want to make your own playbook with special moves for a team or its players to use during practice and competition.

Mental Math

Sports fans know many facts about their favorite teams, the individual players, the history of their favorite sports, and the rules. Athletic cards are often prized by sports fans because they have information printed on their backs to summarize the careers of individual players and the teams for which they played. Fans use this information to calculate in their head about plays and potential performances. The ability to do mathematical figuring (addition, subtraction, multiplication, or division) without writing the information down and keeping all of the data in one's mind is called *mental math*.

Directions

Using mental math, solve the problem below. Then, using a paper and pencil, show how you figured out your answer.

- Think of the number of players necessary for a baseball team.
- Add the number of strikes to put a batter out.
- Subtract the number of balls that forces a batter to walk.
- Subtract the number of outs a team is allowed in an inning.
- What is your final answer?

Thinking Quests

- Make up at least five mental math problems using facts from games and sports. You should have at least 1 one-step problem, 2 two-step problems, and 3 five-step problems. Write down the solutions to your problems and then share your problems with your friends.

- Use sports trading cards (baseball cards, football cards, etc.) to make up your own mental math problems. Have your problems use each of the four mathematical operations (addition, subtraction, multiplication, and division). Write down the solutions so you can check your answers and then share your mental math problems with your friends.

Knowledge of the Game

In order for athletes to succeed at the professional level, they must have a strong understanding of their sport. This includes knowledge about the equipment, players and people involved, and rules of the game. It is also important to know the history of the sport. At various times and for various reasons, some sports change their rules, equipment, or even participants. For example, the sport of whitewater rafting today has several focuses. People participate in these trips to learn about water hydraulics and navigation, water safety and rescue, wilderness knowledge and skills, and leadership and team building.

Directions

Classify the whitewater rafting words into one of the four categories below.

boils chute clean drop eddy ferry gradient hole guide hydraulics keeper pool-drop put-in river rat scout section strainer take-out technical throw bag volume run current river right river left river rating flow high water low water rapid lateral sieve haystack paddle bow stern dry bag life jacket trip leader paddle captain flotilla portage high side wrap swimmer gorp swimmer's position

Equipment	Maneuvers	Environment	People

Thinking Quests

- Look at each of the items listed under the categories above. How have these categories changed over time? For example, what improvements have been made to the equipment over the last 50 years? 100 years? Do people watch or participate for the same reasons they did when the game first began? Were there financial incentives to perform well when the game first started? Have the rules of the game changed? If so, how? Are the rules the same for both male and female teams?

- Think of another sport or game. Make a list of at least 20 items needed to play it. Make your own categories in which the items can be placed. Let a friend classify your words into the appropriate categories. Then, identify how that sport has changed over time. What has made the activity better or safer? What has made the game more challenging? Explain your answers.

If You Build It, They Will Come

Most large cities have some type of professional sports team or league—baseball, basketball, hockey, football, or even soccer. Sports teams change locations and names on a regular basis. This can be due to sponsorship (companies giving money to support the team) or through community commitment (building of stadiums or practice fields). For example, in 1995, the Los Angeles Rams football team moved from California to Missouri and became the St. Louis Rams. Sports teams are also organized in a way that allows them to compete in an organized schedule. These are called *conferences*. Conferences are groups of teams that play one another. Winners of the conference titles then come together to play for national titles. We know some of these games as the Super Bowl and the World Series.

Directions

Many cities have major league or minor league baseball teams. In this activity, you will investigate to find out which cities have teams. Find out what city is the home of each of the following baseball teams. It may be helpful to look in reference books or check the sports pages of the newspaper or Internet sites. For example, Baseball-Reference.com (http://www.baseball-reference.com) has a lot of information about all the various baseball teams. The Official Site of Major League Baseball (http://www.mlb.com) posts statistics, standings, schedules, and players for major league baseball teams.

1. Orioles _____
2. Blue Jays _____
3. Red Sox _____
4. Tigers _____
5. Yankees _____
6. Pirates _____
7. Cardinals _____
8. Royals _____
9. Reds _____
10. Dodgers _____

Thinking Quests

- Using the map of the U.S. in the Appendix, locate each of the cities with a professional team of your choice. Then, identify the conference the team is in. For example, if you were identifying cities with hockey teams, you might color all of the states with the teams in the Southwest conference green. Identify the conferences and colors using a key on your map.

- Select at least five teams from your lists above. Then, track the history of those teams. Make a timeline and identify where the teams first started, if they moved, why they moved locations, and if the name of their team changed over time. What other things about your team changed? The mascot? The team colors? Why do you think certain teams changed and others did not? Explain your answer.

Event Schedules

There are a variety of sports that can be played during the summer. It is difficult to participate in all of them, and practice often requires a schedule. Most schools have sporting schedules for when events and practices will take place, some coming earlier in a season than others. Often times, these schedules are based on weather and available daylight for practice.

Directions

Imagine that you are the activities director for a school and are responsible for organizing the sports schedule. First, on a separate sheet of paper, put the sporting activities in alphabetical order. Then, identify by numerical ranking the sport that would come first, second, and so on throughout the year. Then, for each ranking, give two reasons for why you made the decision you did. For example, swimming may come first because you can practice at an indoor pool, or swimming may be last if you only have an outdoor pool. Before you begin, it may be helpful to think about your geographical location, as this will make a difference in when you can begin the various sports.

---

ski jumping   baseball   soccer   rugby   basketball   rowing
biathlon   gymnastics   canoeing/kayaking   cricket
curling   wrestling   speed skating   boxing   diving
Alpine skiing   fencing   sailing   field hockey   taekwondo
table tennis   water polo   freestyle skiing   archery   hockey
luge   motor sports   softball   pentathlon   Nordic combined
rodeo   cross-country skiing   badminton   shooting
snow boarding   equestrian   football   cycling   swimming
synchronized swimming   figure skating   track and field
triathlon   bobsled   volleyball   beach volleyball
tennis   handball   weightlifting   lacrosse   judo

Thinking Quests

- Identify at least 10 fall/winter sports and make a fall sporting schedule. What new factors did you have to take into consideration? Taking one of the schedules (either fall or summer), make a list of potential games (home and away) for the various sports. What challenges do you face?

- Make a schedule for the next Olympic games. What events do you need to include? In what order should they occur? How many teams get to participate? Did you make separate categories for both women's and men's events? Where should the games take place? Why?

- Look over the different sporting events available at past Olympic games. What activities have the longest history with the Olympics? What activities are the most recent additions to the games? Are there any activities that are not currently a part of the games, but were present at an earlier time? Why do you think these changes occurred? Is it fair to have new sports added? Are all countries able to be represented in all of the sports? Construct your own hypothesis and explain your findings.

Sports Time

Sports commentators on radio and television use specific and vivid verbs to describe the action taking place during a game. These people are able to improvise or think on their feet. They can communicate what is happening in a way that allows listeners or readers to imagine both the action on the field or court and the reaction of the crowd. For example, a sports commentator might say, "It's the last 15 seconds. The Wizards and Lakers are tied for the finals. Pressure is tense. You can hear the crowd pounding the bleachers with their feet. Wait . . . Jordan stole the ball. He's dribbling down the court at a rapid pace. Pass to Jeffries. Jeffries is eyeing the basket. He takes a jump shot. The ball is flying through the air, the ball touches the rim, but doesn't go in. The crowd is screaming. Jordan rebounds the ball and slams it into the basket. Two points to the Wizards! The Wizards are ahead! The crowd is going wild! The clock is down to the last 5 seconds."

Directions

Pretend to be a sports broadcaster commentating for a hockey game. The teams (the Iguanas and the Razorbacks) are close in scores. The Iguanas are down by only one goal. There are only 2 minutes left in the game. A player from the Iguanas has to shoot a penalty shot—a rare thing in hockey. Tell how the game ends. Use the words in the box below in your description of the game.

puck	goalie	forward	guard	center	pad	stick	boards
check	penalty	shot	score	slap shot	skate	face-off	
off sides	back hand	wrist shot	crease	referee			

Thinking Quests

- Select a different game or sport and be the announcer (tennis match, soccer game, swimming race, gymnastics). It may be helpful to practice using a real game with the volume muted on the TV set. How did your tone of voice impact how your audience interpreted the event? Did you use any verbs that were specific to the sport? How did you incorporate facts of the game into your description of the plays? What types of things did you have to balance in your description?

- Write a commentary on the participants during an extreme adventure sport or an adventure race: BMX bike racing, skiing, snowboarding, surfing, kayaking, or motocross. Discuss an athlete's career history, role or actions during the competition, and dedication to the sports community. Research information about this athlete on the Internet and through books at your library.

Leave No Trace

Recreation is part of our daily lives. Outdoor activities, such as hiking, horseback riding, mountain biking, picnicking, climbing, and camping, allow us to enjoy the natural environment. While participating in outdoor recreational activities (both on land and in the water), we may make an impact on the surrounding environment. For example, jet skis and wave runners are commonly used along lakeshores and seashores; however, the sounds made from these watercrafts may scare birds away from their nests and cause stress to marine animals. Pollutants, such as fuel and oil, can leak out of these watercrafts and affect the quality of the water and air. Because these machines can go in shallow waters, their motors may produce enough turbulence to damage underwater plants' root systems. In attempting to keep the environment in as good or better condition than it was in when we arrived, the idea of "Leave No Trace" is commonly practiced by those who participate in outdoor activities, focusing specifically on walks, fires, camping, garbage, cleaning, nature calls, and common courtesy.

Directions

The following guidelines are part of the "Leave No Trace" practices (see http://www.lnt.org). Identify an outdoor sport or activity and discuss why these guideline are important and what you can do to make a difference.

1. Plan ahead and prepare.

2. Travel and camp on durable surfaces.

3. Dispose of waste properly.

4. Leave what you find.

5. Minimize campfire impacts.

6. Respect wildlife.

7. Be considerate of other visitors.

Thinking Quests

- There are a variety of locations in which outdoor activities and sports can take place. Consider the following questions and make a presentation on the idea of "Leave No Trace" and its relationship to outdoor activities. Is it important to have certain activities take place in specific locations? How is this good or bad for the environment? Should there be different rules from those currently in place for how we use parks? Should outdoor activities only be allowed on manmade surfaces? Is the idea of "Leave No Trace" helpful or harmful?

- Make a diagram that shows the relationship among visitors in outdoor environments, the resources in those environments, and the people in charge of those areas. It may be helpful if you select one outdoor activity and look at the relationships among the three areas. Describe the needs of each. Explain how the idea of "Leave No Trace" works to encourage society to plan, travel, and think about how their actions might impact the environment.

Sports and Outdoor Activities Generalizations

If you had 5 minutes to tell someone about sports and outdoor activities, what would you say? This is a difficult task, even for people who study recreational activities and sports for a living. When thinking about the theme of Sports and Outdoor Activities, there are often important ideas we can take away that will help us to think about and remember the role of sports and activities. These important ideas are called *generalizations*. Generalizations are based on factual information or basic understandings of the topic you are studying. An example of a generalization for this theme is: "Sports and outdoor activities take many forms." Generalizations should be written as a conclusion or final thought that can be proved or disproved with support from information you found while researching the topic. Using generalizations to explain a topic or idea can help you to get the main points across in a quick and easy manner. Once you get the main idea across, details can be added that provide support to your ideas.

Directions

Write at least five generalizations about the theme of Sports and Outdoor Activities.

1. _____

_____

2. _____

_____

3. _____

_____

4. _____

_____

5. _____

_____

Thinking Quests

- In what ways do sports and outdoor activities impact the way we live? At home? At school? At work? At play? In our state? In our country? In our continent? In the world? Our environment? In what ways are these impacts the same? In what ways are these impacts different?

- How have your understandings of sports and outdoor activities changed throughout these activities? Identify at least three ideas or questions that need to be considered in the future.

Parks and Forests

This Land is Your Land

Yellowstone was the world's first national park. Created in 1872 by an act of Congress, this area was established as an area set aside under protection of the law for people to enjoy and benefit from its natural resources. As more parks were created, the National Park Service helped to manage the needs of these different areas around the U.S. More specifically, the Park Service worked to conserve scenery, natural and historic objects, and indigenous wildlife, while balancing the need to provide opportunities for visitors to enjoy, but not harm, the ecosystem. The National Park System contains more than 385 different sites, such as national parks, national monuments, seashores, recreational areas, historic and military sites, and battlefields. All of these sites together cover more than 83 million acres and are symbolic of American heritage.

Directions

Using the terms below, identify at least one example of the following and find its location on the map in the Appendix. The National Park System Web site (http://www.eparks.org/about_npca/park_system/a_to_c.asp) may be a helpful resource. It identifies the different types of park systems in alphabetical order, by designation, and by state.

---

international historic site   national battlefield

national battlefield park   national battlefield site

national historical park   national historic site

national lakeshore   national monument   national memorial

national military park   national park   national parkway

national preserve   national reserve   national river

national recreational area   national seashore

national scenic trail   wild and scenic river

unit without designation

Thinking Quests

- There are many different types of parks. Make a chart and explain the characteristics of each type of park. For example, how are national parkways and preserves different from national reserves and parks? What are the differences among national battlefields, battlefield parks, and battlefield sites? Give two additional examples for each designation.

- Each state has its own history that makes it unique. Identify the different types of national park systems in your state and research the historical information for at least three different locations. What do they all have in common? How are they different? Why were they designated as part of the park system? If your state does not have any areas designated as part of the national park system, locate at least two different locations that you believe should be included. Why have these been overlooked? Explain.

Keeping in Tune With Nature

The main goal of the National Park Service is to keep and maintain specific locations for future generations. This goal involves respect for the environment (land, animals, plants) and protection of both cultural and historical artifacts (buildings, antiques, heirlooms). Forest reserves, today called *national forests*, were areas set aside in the late 1800s to protect trees from excessive logging. Today, more than 155 national forests cover more than 187 million acres. This land, originally set aside with the intention to protect the environment and preserve it for future generations, constantly faces challenges: eco- and adventure tourism, wildfires, personal watercrafts (jet skis and wave runners), snowmobiles, toxic chemicals, and climate changes. Advertising campaigns, such as Smokey the Bear and Woodsy the Owl, have been designed to help make the public aware of these challenges. For example, Smokey reminds us "Only YOU can prevent wildfires!"

Directions

Identify if the following facts about these advertising campaigns are true or false using books and the Internet.

_____ Smokey the Bear became the mascot for forest fire prevention during World War II.

_____ Woodsy the Owl encourages kids to form positive relationships with nature.

_____ Bambi was the original mascot for fire prevention.

_____ Woodsy the Owl's motto is "Lend a Hand—Care for the Land!"

_____ Smokey the Bear is based on an actual black bear found after a wildfire in New Mexico.

_____ Both Smokey the Bear and Woodsy the Owl are symbols for the Forest Service.

_____ The original poster of Smokey showed a bear pouring water on a campfire.

_____ Woodsy the Owl is known to say, "Give a hoot. Don't pollute."

Thinking Quests

- Consider the challenges facing national parks and forests. Identify one of those issues and create your own unique mascot and motto to help increase public awareness of the problem. Draw a picture of your mascot and make a poster of your prevention symbol. Identify how your mascot relates to the challenge. Why is this animal or icon the best one for the job? Because your mascot will be educating people, what five things would it emphasize? Support your decision with evidence from newspaper, magazine, or Internet articles. Share your creations.

- Write a song or poem about the challenges faced by the National Forest Service. Include the different ways the animals and plants feel when fires, logging, and other forms of damage to the environment occur. Come up with at least three different ideas the animals and plants have about ways to resolve these challenges. Feel free to use musical instruments as sound effects. For example, a kazoo could be used for the sound of a chainsaw used during logging, drums could be the footsteps of a bear, or maracas could be a snake. Share your poem with your friends.

On the Loose

At least 87 species of animals have become extinct in North America since 1600. In order to protect endangered and threatened animals, refuges have been established. In 1903, Theodore Roosevelt created the first national wildlife refuge to protect breeding birds at Pelican Island in Florida. Refuges originally helped to protect animals that were overhunted, such as bison and egrets. When the climate changed, refuges helped to protect these animals by providing a nourishing and safe environment. Today, the National Wildlife Refuge System has more than 547 different locations and consists of more than 93 million acres. The role of the refuges changes depending on the breeding success of the animals living there. For example, at certain times, once-threatened animals may be hunted in regulated amounts. However, refuges continue to be challenged by the development of surrounding lands. As businesses and industries move closer to the refuges, the ecosystems become polluted, animals are displaced, and diseases spread as the population density increases. Scientists and researchers study these effects to determine the healthy ratios among these competing systems.

Directions

Select a National Wildlife Refuge location and identify the animals that live there. Make a food web showing what the various animals eat and who or what gets eaten. Some items on your web may be eaten by a lot of different things. Put these at the bottom of your web. Other animals on your web may be the prey of only one or two different predators. Put these animals at the top of your web. Draw arrows that show the progression and hierarchy for your refuge. How do all of these living things work together to create an ecosystem?

Thinking Quests

- Identify the challenges your refuge faces and cover the plants and animals that would be impacted by one of those challenges. What happens to your ecosystem? Can a new balance be found? What will happen to certain species? Why? Explain your answer and draw a picture of what your refuge would look like before and after the change to your environment.

- Populations change in both positive and negative ways. The numbers of animals in a species can increase if there are more births than deaths, and the numbers may decrease if there are more deaths than births. This relationship between births and deaths over time impacts the population density, that is, how many animals are able to live in a certain area. Look back at your food web and identify what would happen if the environment changed so that not as many of a certain species lived. What would happen if too many lived? How would that impact your web? What impact would this have on your ecosystem? What can researchers and scientists do to help maintain this balance? Are plants or animals able to do anything to help maintain this balance?

Land Management

There are a variety of governmental agencies that look after national lands: the National Park Service, the National Park System, the National Forest System, the Department of Agriculture, the National Wildlife Refuge, U.S. Fish and Wildlife Service, and the Bureau of Land Management. Many of these agencies are hierarchical, that is, they are a smaller part of another department or system. For example, the National Forest System is managed by the Department of Agriculture. These agencies often work together with a similar purpose or goal in mind. However, differences in opinions may result in disagreements in how lands should be managed. For example, the Bureau of Land Management (BLM) regulates approximately 264 million acres. This is more than any other federal agency. BLM lands are used for grazing, logging, mining, and public recreation; however, there are many controversies about how the land should be used, especially regarding grazing and logging.

Directions

Research the different types of governmental agencies and environmental groups and make a chart or graph that shows the relationships (hierarchical, similarities, differences) among them. For example, because the National Forest System is governed by the Department of Agriculture, the Department of Agriculture could be larger or above the National Forest System. Then, identify a challenge faced by these departments and describe what perspective each office might have on how to solve the problem. Why do you think there are different perspectives? Why are there similar perspectives? What common ground do all of these agencies share? What are the main differences?

Thinking Quests

- Using the map in the Appendix, identify the different federal lands (National Park System, National Forest System, Bureau of Land Management) in the U.S. Color each land type a different color and make a key. Locate three of the oldest parks, forests, and areas governed by the Bureau of Land Management. Why do you think these were originally selected? In what ways are these places managed by the different governmental agencies?

- Using the list of nine areas you selected above, plan a vacation where you would visit at least three of these sites. Who would you take? Where would you start and end? What supplies would you need? How much would it cost? Determine your daily mileage (how many miles you will travel each day) and then calculate the cost of gas, food, lodging, admission to the parks, tourist memorabilia, and so forth. The Internet may be helpful in calculating several of the expenses, planning your trip, and identifying stopping points along the way.

Setting Boundaries

In geography, boundaries are generally considered to be a line that separates two areas. Examples of boundaries can be rivers, mountain ranges, state lines, changes in plant life, and even highways or roads. Boundaries can be created by the environment, or they can be manmade. When a boundary is manmade, it can have an impact on the environment and cause habitat fragmentation. This occurs when a naturally occurring habitat is subdivided into smaller parts for housing subdivisions and farmland. Even if small parts of a habitat are changed, they can have lasting effects on the animals and plants living in that area. Some birds and parasites prey on bird eggs and their young by living on the edges of habitats. Building roads and clearing trees for power lines in forested areas increases the area in which these predators may live while simultaneously making the original inhabitants of the area vulnerable to extinction.

Directions

Identify the threats each of the following animals pose due to habitat fragmentation. Identify where these animals typically live and what can be done to help reduce the problem posed by these predators.

> brown-headed cowbird   bronzed cowbird   shiny cowbird
>
> coyote   raccoon   skunk   crow   blue jays   mute swan

Thinking Quests

- Select two of the animals listed above and make a diagram that explains the relationship among the following: manmade boundaries, predators, original habitat, new habitat, and original habitat species. How does this change impact the ecosystem? How do these changes impact migration patterns of different animals? Explain and support your answers.

- Make a list of criteria you believe the park/forest should follow for placement of manmade boundaries (roads, parking lots, trails, lodges, play areas). Share your ideas with your friends. Using your list, select three different national parks and forests. For each location, use your list to evaluate the choice and placement of manmade boundaries. What decisions were good? What decisions were poor? How many subdivisions were created? Are any animals becoming extinct or endangered in the park or forest? What impact do the boundaries make in each area? What would you change? Using one of the parks or forests you researched, design a new route. Have your friends give you feedback on your newly designed path.

- How do boundaries impact the reintroduction of animals to a specific habitat? Research the success of the reintroduction of the wolf and the bald eagle. How are these experiments similar? How are they different? Why did these efforts work or not work? Explain.

Environmental Design

Parks and forests come in a variety of shapes, sizes, types, and locations. When the national lands are set aside for parks and forests, planning has to occur at every step of the process. If roads or trails are not maintained, then damage may occur to the plants and animals living in that area. In addition, it is important for developers to have a strong understanding of the needs of each individual park or forest as designing requires planning, understanding of the situation, and the knowledge of the area in which the design will take place.

Directions

Design your own national park or forest. Identify the types of boundaries, its location, and why people like to go there. Make a map or diorama of what the park or forest would look like. Explain why you designed it the way you did.

Possible things to include:

walking trails   beach   picnic areas   restrooms   areas to camp

information desks   plants, shrubbery   flowers   places to sit

playground equipment   materials needed   fences   signs

rocks/stones   nature preserve

Thinking Quests

- Assign a cost to each of these items you put in your park. What natural resources could you use to cut back on costs? How much would it cost to get your park or forest into working condition? Find out how much it costs to maintain three different parks or forests. How does this compare to what you calculated? Did you include salaries for park and forest rangers?

- Research the national parks and forests for states in two different geographical locations. Make a map of these states and identify these locations. Research at least three parks or forests in each state and identify why people like to go there. Make a map of the park or forest and then research the challenges each of these resources faces, such as pollution, deforestation, fires, and the effects of tourism. How are the state and national government systems helping each of these locations? Do they provide employees, have environmental laws, or give financial support? Design a flyer or poster that would help make the community aware of the attractions and challenges these parks and forests face.

Adventure Stories

Travelers have stories to share about their adventures. The story of Beck Weathers and his experiences on Mount Everest on May 10, 1996, is a shining example of courage and of determination. Part of a climbing crew expedition to the top of Everest, Weathers and the other members of the climbing crew faced extreme blizzard conditions. Nine climbers died on the peak, and Weathers' body was among those left for dead. After lying 18 hours in the extreme subzero elements, he awoke from a deep hypothermic coma and found his way back to camp.

Directions

Use the morphological matrix below to create many different stories by combining the categories in various ways. Different words have been selected for each of the categories typically found in an adventure story. Randomly select seven different numbers that range from 1 to 5. The numbers represent words for each category. For example, if the numbers 1, 2, 2, 3, 4, 2, and 5 were selected, then your story would include: a prospector, canoeing, the Nile River, Rock Hopper Penguin tracks, the dilemma of man vs. man, and a fear of deep water. Create at least three different stories.

	Character	Physical Activity	Travel Locations	Animal Track	Weather Condition	Dilemma	Fear
1	Prospector	Hiking	Yellowstone	The Big Bad Wolf	Blizzard	Man vs. self	Heights
2	Tourist	Canoeing	Nile River	Stegasaurous	Rainy	Man vs. man	Spiders
3	Goldilocks	Rock climbing	Ayers Rock, Australia	Rock hopper penguin	Windy	Man vs. environment	The dark
4	Kyack instructor	Mountain biking	Niagara Falls	Gila monster	Hot	Man vs. society	Elephants
5	Forest ranger	Swimming	Sahara Desert	Moose	Calm	Man vs. time	Deep water

Thinking Quests

- Make your own morphological matrix and create at least three of your own stories. Feel free to add new topics to the matrix. When writing your story, make sure to describe the environment, add details to the main character, and tell us about his or her specific adventures.

- Add a twist to your story by allowing the reader to make the decision for the main character. This can be done by presenting some information in your story and then giving the reader a choice of two or three different options to determine what happens next. For example, if the prospector decided to follow penguin tracks into a cave, then the reader could go to one page. If the prospector decided to instead canoe down the Nile River, then the reader could go to another page. In this way, the readers are selecting the plot of the story and choosing the fate of the main character.

It's Debatable

Protecting the environment is an issue with which many of us are concerned. However, there are a variety of ideas for how this should happen. These differences in opinion are often called *controversial issues* or *hot topics*, as there is no obviously right or wrong way for the issue to be resolved. The idea of logging national parks and forests is extremely controversial. Demonstrations, sit-ins, flyers, protests, debates, books, and TV, radio, or Internet coverage may capture the tension of these deeply felt feelings. Becoming knowledgeable about the different points of view will help you to make informed decisions on what you think is the best solution to the issue.

Directions

Select one of the following controversial issues and debate it. Identify the positive and negative points in each perspective. Identify the people involved and those who are impacted by the decisions.

> Logging in national parks/forests
>
> Controlled burns in national parks/forests
>
> Hunting in national parks/forests
>
> Use of motorcrafts in national parks/forests
>
> Limiting the number of visitors to national parks/forests
>
> Reintroduction of endangered species into national parks/forests
>
> Drilling/mining for natural resources in national parks/forests
>
> Involvement of Native Americans in national parks/forests

Thinking Quests

- Select five different national parks or forests. For each, identify at least three challenges it faces and explain what could be done to help combat them. Design a plan that would help one of the parks or forests. Present your ideas by explaining how your design would help to solve the problem, why it would work, and who could get involved. You will also need to calculate how much your program would cost and how long it would take to implement.

- Select two of the controversial issues listed above and identify the various perspectives from at least eight different organizations and groups. Create your own ranking system to categorize the groups' perspectives. This system could be based on group size, political affiliation, environmental stance, age, and so forth. What are the characteristics of the people involved in each group? Identify any patterns you notice. What general statements can you make about all of the groups involved? In what specific ways do the groups differ in opinion?

What a Resource

Timber, fresh water, mineral deposits . . . What do these things have in common? They are all considered natural resources. Natural resources are materials, typically holding some value or wealth, found in their natural state. There are many types of resources. Resources can provide support or assistance (such as a person, book, or tool), they can be stored for future use (such as grain, money, or even knowledge), and they can be used for profit (such as oil, sugar, and salt). The idea of something being a resource depends on where you live. For example, some cultures do not value resources that others find important or necessary for survival. This difference in opinion is often referred to as an ethic, or a set of standards and rules that guide what we believe to be right and wrong. In the United States, there are two main ethics that conflict in their views on natural resources. The frontier ethic is based on the idea that humans are separate from nature. According to the frontier ethic, resources are unlimited and should be consumed, humans do not have to obey natural laws, and human success is determined by the amount of control they have over the natural environment. The opposing view is called the sustainable development ethic. According to this alternative perspective, society should meet its needs without placing limits on future generations. Three main points that describe the focus of the sustainable development ethic are: resources are limited and are not all meant for consumption, humans are part of nature and should obey natural laws, and human success is reliant upon living in harmony with the natural environment.

Directions

With several other students, divide into groups and debate the following issues from the frontier ethic and the sustainable development ethic perspectives.

- Using coal as fuel.

- Clearing rain forests for ranch land.

- Running water while brushing your teeth.

- Using public transportation (busses, trains, subways).

- Buying oil from underdeveloped countries.

Thinking Quests

- Look around your local community and find evidence of the frontier ethic. How do these examples support the three main ideas behind this perspective? Why do you think people believe in the frontier ethic? Why do you think people practice the frontier ethic? Identify areas in your community that support the sustainable development ethic. How do these examples support the three main ideas behind this perspective? Why do you think people believe in the sustainable development perspective? Interview several community members and ask them to describe any changes in their personal practices over the past 20 years. What has influenced their ethical decisions? Write a report of your findings and share it with your peers.

- Consider the name "frontier ethic." Why do you think this ethic is named in this manner? Look back over the explorations and conquests that have occurred throughout the world. What role do conflicts over resources play in these struggles for power? Research at least two different explorations or conquests. Identify the people in power, the resources under conflict, the struggle that occurred, and the impact the struggle had on both the environment and those involved. Has this struggle been resolved? In your opinion, was this the best way to resolve this issue? Why or why not? How would these conflicts change if society viewed resources through a sustainable development perspective?

Parks and Forests
Generalizations

If you had 5 minutes to tell someone about parks and forests, what would you say? This is a difficult task, even for people who study parks and forests for a living. When thinking about the theme of Parks and Forests, there are often important ideas we can take away that will help us to think about and remember the role of parks and forests. These important ideas are called *generalizations*. Generalizations are based on factual information or basic understandings of the topic you are studying. An example of a generalization for this theme is: "Parks and Forests take many forms." Generalizations should be written as a conclusion or final thought that can be proved or disproved with support from information you found while researching the topic. Using generalizations to explain a topic or idea can help you to get the main points across in a quick and easy manner. Once you get the main idea across, details can be added that provide support to your ideas.

Directions

Write at least five generalizations about the theme of Parks and Forests.

1. _____

_____

2. _____

_____

3. _____

_____

4. _____

_____

5. _____

_____

Thinking Quests

- In what ways do parks and forests impact the way we live? At home? At school? At work? At play? In our state? In our country? In our continent? In the world? Our environment? In what ways are these impacts the same? In what ways are these impacts different?

- How have your understandings of parks and forests changed throughout these activities? Identify at least three ideas or questions that need to be considered in the future.

Weather

Weather Words

There are many different words that describe weather. Weather looks at the state of the atmosphere at a specific time and place. Weather consists of variables such as temperature, moisture, wind speed, and barometric pressure. The combination of specific variables changes the conditions of our surroundings. For example, an outside temperature in the mid-80s with a lot of moisture in the air and a high wind speed may bring warnings and watches for thunderstorms. However, these same conditions, depending on the geographic location, may bring a short burst of rain showers. For this reason, weather is described in many different ways. The words we use are dependent on the type of information needed: general forecast, severe weather, non-precipitation, hydraulics and flooding, ocean or marine locations, and so forth.

Directions

Create your own categories for the following list of weather terms. The National Weather Service Forecast Office Web site (http://www.crh.noaa.gov/lmk/terms.htm) may be a useful reference.

---

acid rain   advection   advisory   air mass   altocumulus   alsostratus
anemometer   anticyclone   anvil   atmosphere   barometer   blowing dust
bow echo   ceiling   cirrus   climate   cold front   condensation   coriolis force
cumulonimbus   cumulus cloud   cut off low   cyclone   dew   dew point
Doppler radar   downburst   drizzle   dry line   dust devil   El Niño   flood stage
fog   freezing level   freezing rain   front   frost   funnel cloud
geostationary satellite   GOES   greenhouse effect   ground fog   gust   gust front
hail   halos   haze   high   humidity   hurricane   Indian summer   inversion
isobar   jet stream   knot   lapse rate   lightning   low   macroburst
measurable   mesocyclone   meteorology   microburst   millibar   Nexrad   NOAA
weather radio   occluded front   orographic uplift   outflow   overcast
overshooting top   ozone   precipitation   pressure   radar   radiosonde   rain
rainbow   relative humidity   ridge   scattered clouds   severe thunderstorm
shelf cloud   shower   sleet   snow   snow flurries   squall line   stationary front
straight line winds   stratosphere   stratus   subsidence   subtropical jet   supercell
sustained winds   thermal   thunder   thunderstorm   tornado   trace
trade winds   tropical depression   tropical disturbance   tropical storm
troposphere   trough   turbulence   virga   visibility   vorticity   wall cloud

---

Thinking Quests

- Illustrate one of the weather categories you made above. Research how all of the items in your category are interrelated. What conditions have to exist for this type of weather to occur? How should people prepare? Is there any reason for concern about this type of weather? Present your findings.

- Using the information you found above in your research about a specific weather category, assume the role of a meteorologist. Pretend your local community is experiencing this type of weather. Discuss the current weather conditions, the impact the weather is having on the local community, and offer predictions for the weather pattern. Create a video of your weather forecast and share it with your peers.

North Winds

Meteorologists must have a careful eye when forecasting weather. They have to keep track of the temperature, barometric pressure, and wind speeds. In order to be accurate in their forecasts, meteorologists have to pay close attention to many different details. A word find is a great game that helps train our eyes to look for things that are around us. It encourages us to look for things we could easily overlook.

Directions

Use the words listed in the box below to complete the word find. Words are placed vertically, horizontally, backwards, and on the diagonal. Letters can be used more than once, and the words may overlap. Circle the letters that form words. You will not use every letter in every box.

freezing	U N T M O W H H A T S K E
ski	M I T T E N S K N A K I F
storm	B R U C Y I T H N O I E R
drop	R A I N Z N O R T H S G E
sled	E K C J U D R W Q R T Y E
icicle	L K I L S P M U D O I U Z
umbrella	L J C O L D H G R F D S I
mittens	A C L X E A S N O W M A N
snowman	V B E N D M A S P D R T G
hats	I N O W S P U M N E C I B
rain	
ice	
north	
mud	

Thinking Quests

- Create a list of 20 weather-related words and make your own word find. Your word find can have a theme, such as "Winter" or "Hurricane Season." Make a copy of this and use it as an answer key. Then, have your friends try to find the weather names within your game.

- Using your list of 20 words, create a crossword puzzle. For example, the clue for "umbrella" could be "held over head in rain." Make a copy of your puzzle and use it as an answer key. Then, have your friends try to find the correct words to fill it in.

WORD FIND
Created by _____

The Weather Today . . .

I t has often been said that in order to understand the future we must understand the past. *The Farmer's Almanac* keeps track of weather patterns and offer suggestions on the best times for planting and harvesting crops, as well as what the general growing season will be like. This almanac is based on past weather conditions in the United States. Detailed records about rain, temperature, and weather patterns are compared to crop productions or yields. This data is a guide for farmers about what crops may be best to plant.

Directions

Examine what the weather is like for one city on each of the seven continents for 2 weeks. Record the high and low temperature for the day, the time of the sunrise and sunset, the fullness of the moon, and the amount of rain for the day. Then, create your own weather symbols and use them to identify the general forecast for the day. For example, you might draw a sun for warm and sunny days and a darkened cloud for cloudy days. After 2 weeks of records, what upcoming patterns can you predict? Identify the similarities and differences. What had the largest impact on the differences from one location to another? Why?

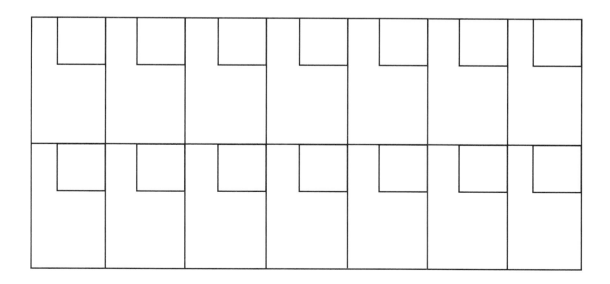

Thinking Quests

- Meteorologists use scientific instruments to help them predict the weather. Research the different types of instruments used to predict weather. The National Weather Service Web site (http://nws.noaa.gov) may be a helpful reference. How have these tools changed over time? Before there were these types of tools, how was weather predicted?

- There are many urban legends on how to tell a storm is coming. Some people say you can smell a storm coming, others say they can feel it in their joints. Can animals sense an upcoming storm? Farmers often say that cattle turn their backs to the upcoming winds, and cat owners notice their pets wanting to come inside. Is it possible to sense weather changes? Find research to support your opinion and debate this issue with your peers.

It Depends

There is a variety of factors that impact what we wear when we get up in the morning. Some people watch the weather forecasts, some people step outside to get a feel for the temperature, and others just put on what is clean. If it is cold outside, athletes will often wear clothes that are tight against their skin in order to keep a layer of body heat near them. Once they warm up from exercise, their external body temperature can rise as much as 20 degrees. For example, if it is 30 degrees Fahrenheit outside and a runner is warmed up, she will actually feel like it is 50 degrees outside. This makes a dramatic difference in the types of clothing that are needed at the beginning and end of a work out.

Directions

Set a timer for 10 minutes and, with a friend, brainstorm a list of as many different types of ideas as you can for one of the suggestions below. When the timer dings, share your thoughts with the other person. Put a star next to the ideas that your friend does not have on his or her list. These ideas are considered unique or original.

1. Things to take to the beach on a hot day.
2. Things to wear in winter in the northern states.
3. Reasons people like snow.
4. How storms (rain or snow) can be harmful.
5. Things to do on a hot day; a rainy day.
6. Changes that seasons bring.

Thinking Quests

- There are many different sayings we have to express weather. The phrase "a toad-choker rain" is used to express rain showers that last for a short period of time and come down so quickly that the ground cannot absorb all of the moisture. Make up five of your own weather sayings and draw pictures that illustrate the idea in a cartoonish manner.

- The phrase "April showers bring May flowers" is frequently used to talk about the weather needs of plants. Research the role weather plays in plant growth and in the various seasons. Why are hard frosts needed? Why are wet springs helpful? Does weather impact how much sap can come from maple trees? How about when leaves change colors in the fall?

Climate Patterns

The Earth's climate is made up of several different zones: polar, tropical, and temperate. These zones each have different average temperatures and rainfall patterns, and they are heated in different amounts because the Earth's surface and shape are uneven. While the equator receives the most direct light from the sun, the poles only get angles of light. For this reason, the equator heats quickly, and heat then spreads toward the poles. On the other hand, because the poles do not receive direct light from the sun, they remain much colder and the cold air spreads toward the equator. Temperature zones between the equator and the poles get a mixture of polar and tropical air. In addition, global winds impact the different climate zones. When wind carries moisture from the ocean to the land, it brings water vapor, often creating a marine or wet ecosystem. As wind continues to move across land, the moisture decreases through rainfall. As the wind loses its moisture, the dry air creates arid or desert-like ecosystems.

Directions

Using the world map in the Appendix, color code the polar, temperate, and tropical areas. Identify the similarities and differences among these zones as they relate to temperature and precipitation. Then, answer the following questions.

- Why does warm air hold more moisture than cold air?
- What are the characteristics of the different climate zones?
- In what climate is the United States located?
- Why are many deserts located at 30 degrees latitude?

Thinking Quests

- Construct a model or demonstration that explains how the Earth's shape and surface causes it to heat unevenly. Identify the areas that receive the most direct rays from the sun. Present your findings to your peers.

- Identify the different ways people have adjusted their lifestyles to their environments. Identify at least two different locations per continent and explain how homes are constructed, how people dress, and what people eat. Interview five different people from other climates. Which climate do they prefer? Identify the pros and cons for living in each climate. Research the different world populations. Which countries have the most people? Do you notice any relationship between the locations of these countries and the climate zones? Explain your answers.

Solid, Liquid, Gas

Most weather follows a particular pattern. Wind typically brings clouds, which hold water vapor. When water vapor gets cold in the atmosphere, it changes into crystals or water droplets. As these droplets get bigger and bigger, gravity pulls them toward the Earth and they fall to the ground. Depending on the temperature in the air, they may fall as rain, snow, sleet, or even hail. The upper atmosphere of the Earth is very cold. For this reason, water vapor usually starts out as snow and, as it falls to the Earth's warm surface, it melts into rain. Clouds are made from moisture in the air, the temperature, and the presence of condensation on dust particles. Water condenses (freezes) when the temperature gets colder. In turn, the temperature decreases when there is not as much heat energy within molecules or when barometric pressure changes. Molecules create energy when they bump into one another, and, when they slow down and spread out, they lose heat and energy. At higher elevations, such as in the mountains, there is less pressure, so the air and water molecules thin out. As the molecules spread out, they don't bump into one another as often and lose energy. When water molecules slow down, they change from a vapor or gas into a liquid in the form of condensation. The changing of form for water molecules is called the *dew point*.

Materials

- Duct tape
- 2 large plastic or glass jars
- Rocks
- Sand
- Water

Directions

Place approximately 1–2 inches of sand in the bottom of a plastic or glass jar. Make sure the sand is saturated with water. Put the rocks in the sand. Tape the mouth of the jar to the mouth of an identical jar. Place the jars in a sunny window. Observe the jars several times a day and keep a record of the solar energy, evaporation, condensation, and water level. After observing the jars for a week, summarize your findings and consider the following questions:

- Does condensation occur at certain times of the day?

- What allows condensation to occur?

- What roles do sunlight and temperature play in this process?

Thinking Quests

- Draw a picture of the water cycle that illustrates the interactions of the water molecules, the air molecules, and the water droplets. Create your own experiment to show this cycle and describe why each step occurs. Explain how water vapor is a source of water.

- Identify the various types of precipitation. Describe the characteristics of each form of precipitation and the feelings we associate with them. For example, fog is often considered spooky or mysterious. Find five examples of these descriptions within books. How have authors used these descriptions to set the mood or tone for a book? Write your own story that uses weather to create the setting.

- Make a chart of the different types of clouds. Draw a picture of each and identify its distinguishing characteristics. Does this type of cloud typically bring rain? At what atmospheric level does it sit? What weather patterns are commonly associated with this type of cloud? Share your findings in a presentation.

Down Came the Rain

"Itsy, bitsy spider came up the water spout
Down came the rain and washed the spider out
Out came the sun and dried up all the rain
And the itsy bitsy spider crawled up the spout again"

The song, "Itsy, Bitsy Spider" talks about the collection of water in a certain area and the impact it has on the animals that live there. When it rains outside, puddles, streams, and lakes take up water that runs off from watersheds or higher elevation land areas. Watersheds are typically separated from one another by ridges or mountain divides. When water falls on the top of the divide, it drains or runs off into different watersheds or collection areas. Watersheds occur all around us in parking lots, drainage ditches, and school playgrounds. Puddles in these areas collect the water that runs off from the surrounding area. When puddles overflow or the ground is saturated (especially during toad-choker rains), water that was originally held and collected is released. As water overflows the collection area, it picks up additional materials, such as litter, branches and twigs, leaves, soil, and toxic materials (gasoline, fertilizers, oil). When the water is finally absorbed by the soil, the natural materials decompose. However, the toxic materials can contaminate or endanger our ecosystem. These toxic materials are called *pollutants*.

Directions

Take a field trip or hike and make a map of a specific area you want to study. Identify the buildings, parking lots, playgrounds, trees, grass, gardens, and water sources (streams, ponds, ditches, pipes, etc.). Make a legend or key for your map that identifies the following:

- the direction of water flowing into and away from an area;
- the natural materials that might have been carried into the area;
- areas where water may collect;
- unnatural materials that might have been carried into the area;
- natural items that help slow the flow of water;
- natural materials that could be carried away from the area; and
- unnatural materials that could have been carried away from the area.

Make two copies of your map. Using the first map, take a field trip on a clear day and look carefully at the buildings. Predict on your map where the water from the roof flows and where the other sources of water will go when it rains. Look for additional materials that could be picked up during the rain (both materials that could decompose and materials that could be toxic). Don't forget to check the roofs of surrounding buildings. On a rainy day, use your second map to verify your original water flow patterns. Did your prediction match what you observed? Explain.

Thinking Quests

- Using your maps above, determine the characteristics of water flow that you observed. What slows water? What makes water flow more quickly? Look at a topographical map of the location you studied. Identify the typical water flow patterns within the watershed. Write a report that includes visuals (graphs, charts, maps, photographs) to explain and support your ideas.

- Interview a city planner or engineer and gather information about how your town was developed to deal with water runoff. Gather information about the storm drainage system and where runoff from streets, parking lots, and housing divisions goes. Report on the water management system for your community. How do city planners and engineers try to protect the city from environmental problems, such as pollution and erosion?

Rain, Rain, Go Away

Does it always seem like it is sunny on the days you have school and rainy on the weekends? Have you ever wished that the weather forecast for a particular day was different than what it was—allowing you to wear shorts when it was cold or even snow ski on warm days? Is there anything we can do to influence or control the water cycle? Technology has allowed us to begin taking control of the water cycle. We have built dams to protect us from flooding, covered reservoirs to hold more water, made seed clouds to produce rain, and even made our own snow. However, does the planting of trees and plants help us to control the water cycle?

Materials

- 2 aluminum foil roasting pans
- 2 empty milk containers or buckets
- 1 piece of sod (cut to fit the roasting pan)
- 3-foot board (2 x 4)
- 2 coffee cans or watering cans filled with water
- Scissors
- Stiff paper (tagboard)
- Soil
- Table

Directions

At one end of each aluminum foil roasting pan, cut a v-shaped notch about 1.5 inches deep and place a spout made of stiff paper so that water placed in the container will be able to drain into the container below. Put a piece of sod in the bottom of one pan and bare soil in the bottom of the other. Set both pans on a table and place the board under the end opposite the spout. This will give both pans the same slope. Place the containers or buckets below the spouts to catch the water. Pour the can of water at the same time and from the same height into the same spot into both pans. Observe the following:

- What effect does the sod (plant) have on the water's speed?

- What effect does the sod (plant) have on the amount of runoff on each slope?

- What does the runoff look like for each slope?

- Does the water affect the surface shape of each slope?

Thinking Quests

- Explain your findings. In what ways do plants and trees impact the water cycle? Looking back at your research in Activity 7, what changes would you recommend to the area you studied? Draw a new map that illustrates any changes.

- Interview a horticulturist. How does landscape design impact the water cycle? Should certain plants be placed in certain areas? Why or why not? Explain your answers.

Weather Writer

"In the morning, the dust hung like fog, and the sun was ripe as new blood. All the day dust sifted down from the sky, and the next day it sifted down. An even blanket covered the earth. It settled on the corn, piled up on the tops of fence posts, piled up on the wires; it settled on roofs, blanketed the weeds and trees."

—John Steinbeck, *The Grapes of Wrath*

John Steinbeck, a famous American author, captured the triumphs and tragedies of human life. He lived in Oklahoma during the late 1930s when the Dust Bowl, storms of dust and wind, brought poverty and starvation to farmers and migrant workers. Weather challenges, such as El Niño, floods, and droughts, are faced around the world and throughout time. Wet and dry climatic cycles have occurred on almost every continent. Many years of good crops, regular rainfall, and productive economic exchange can be followed by years of drought. Weather cycles impact thousands of people every year and cause great financial loss and hardship.

Directions

Read the first two chapters of Steinbeck's *The Grapes of Wrath* and research the topic of dust bowls. What perspective does the author take? Do you agree with his presentation of this weather event? What impact did dust bowls have on society? Does the story appear realistic? Explain your ideas with support from the text.

Thinking Quests

- Identify another weather challenge that has recently happened or one that happened in the past. For example, you could study a flood, drought, hurricane, blizzard, or typhoon. Research the impacts this had on the local community and write a story that expresses the drama of the event. Do people have to evacuate? Do some choose to stay and tough it out?

- Research the water-related weather cycles that occur around the world. Are these natural? Can society do anything to help prevent these types of disasters? Design an educational brochure to inform people of prevention techniques. Share your findings with your peers.

Weather Generalizations

f you had 5 minutes to tell someone about weather, what would you say? This is a difficult task, even for people who study weather for a living. When thinking about the theme of weather, there are often important ideas we can take away that will help us to think about and remember the role of weather. These important ideas are called *generalizations*. Generalizations are based on factual information or basic understandings of the topic you are studying. An example of a generalization for this theme is: "Weather takes many forms." Generalizations should be written as a conclusion or final thought that can be proved or disproved with support from information you found while researching the topic. Using generalizations to explain a topic or idea can help you to get the main points across in a quick and easy manner. Once you get the main idea across, details can be added that provide support to your ideas.

Directions

Write at least five generalizations about the theme of Weather.

1. _____

_____

2. _____

_____

3. _____

_____

4. _____

_____

5. _____

_____

Thinking Quests

- In what ways does weather impact the way we live? At home? At school? At work? At play? In our state? In our country? In our continent? In the world? Our environment? In what ways are these impacts the same? In what ways are these impacts different?

- How have your understandings of weather changed throughout these activities? Identify at least three ideas or questions that need to be considered in the future.

Appendices

Appendix 1:
Alignment to National Standards

Geography (K–4) = Geography National Standards (Grades K–4)
Geography (5–8) = Geography National Standards (Grades 5–8)
Social Studies (Early) = Social Studies National Standards (Early Grades)
Social Studies (Middle) = Social Studies National Standards (Middle Grades)
Science (K–4) = National Science Content Standards (Grades K–4)
Science (5–8) = National Science Content Standards (Grades 5–4)
English = Standards for the English Language Arts
Math = Principles and Standards for School Mathematics

Animals

Students will explore the animal classes as described by the five kingdom taxonomic chart. They will investigate the different ecological regions and climactic zones in which animals live and will identify the specific characteristics and features of animals that separate them into species. After researching the basic needs of a variety of animals, students will consider the overlapping relationships between niches and habitats. Further study will involve exploring the names of different animals as they mature and develop.

Activity 1:   Perform a Silent Role

Thinking Skill(s): Collecting & Organizing Data, Observing

Standards:		
	English	4, 12
	Geography (K–4)	1.1, 2.1
	Geography (5–8)	1.1, 2.1
	Science (K–4)	Life Science A
	Science (5–4)	Life Science C
	Social Studies (Early)	3b, 3c,
	Social Studies (Middle)	3b, 3c

Activity 2:   **It's Time to Classify**

Thinking Skill(s): Classifying, Collecting and Organizing Data, Comparing and Contrasting

Standards:		
	Geography (K–4)	1.1, 2.1
	Geography (5–8)	1.1, 2.1
	Science (K–4)	Unifying Concepts and Processes A, Life Science A
	Science (5–8)	Unifying Concepts and Processes A, B, C, Life Science A, C, D
	Social Studies (Early)	3b, 3c, 3e
	Social Studies (Middle)	3b, 3c, 3e

Activity 3:   **Recreate a Shape**

Thinking Skill(s): Comparing and Contrasting, Imagining

Standards:		
	Geography (K–4)	1.1
	Geography (5–8)	1.1
	Science (K–4)	Life Science A
	Science (5–8)	Life Science A

Activity 4:   **Animal Antics**

Thinking Skill(s): Classifying

Standards:		
	English	5, 6

Activity 5:   **A New Ending**

Thinking Skill(s): Imagining

Standards:		
	English	3, 5, 6, 12

Activity 6:   **20 Questions**

Thinking Skill(s): Classifying, Collecting and Organizing Data

Standards:		
	Geography (K–4)	1.1, 2.1
	Geography (5–8)	1.1, 2.1
	Science (K–4)	Life Science A, B, C
	Science (5–8)	Life Science A, B, C, D, E
	Social Studies (Early)	3b, 3c, 3e
	Social Studies (Middle)	3b, 3c, 3e

Activity 7: **"Oh, Give Me a Home"**

Thinking Skill(s): Collecting and Organizing Data, Interpreting

Standards:
Science (K–4)	Life Science C
Science (5–8)	Life Science D
Social Studies (Early)	3c, 3e
Social Studies (Middle)	3c, 3e

Activity 8: **What If . . .**

Thinking Skill(s): Hypothesizing, Imagining

Standards:
English	5, 6

Activity 9: **Baby Names**

Thinking Skill(s): Collecting and Organizing Data

Standards:
Science (K–4)	Unifying Concepts and Processes A
Science (5–8)	Unifying Concepts and Processes A

Activity 10: **Animal Generalizations**

Thinking Skill(s): Summarizing

Flowering Plants

Students will research the names and function of various parts of a flowering plant. They will interview people who work with plants and will create their own experiments regarding plant needs and the developmental growth cycles of different plants. Plant specimen storage will be explored, as well as the symbolic meaning certain plants hold. Students will complete an investigation of their neighborhood or school and will chart the various plants they found. Further study will focus on the characteristics of specific plants, and the benefits or detriments plants bring to society. At the end of this theme, students will create their own ecosystem or biosphere.

Activity 1: **Flower Find**

Thinking Skill(s): Observing

Standards:
English	12

Activity 2: A Flower's Parts

Thinking Skill(s): Collecting and Organizing Data, Hypothesizing

Standards: Science (K–4)   Earth and Space Science A
             Science (5–8)   Earth and Space Science A

Activity 3: Flowering Plant Uses

Thinking Skill(s): Collecting and Organizing Data, Criticizing

Standards: Science (K–4)   History and Nature of Science A
             Science (5–8)   History and Nature of Science A, B
             Social Studies (Early) 7e

Activity 4: Watch Them Grow

Thinking Skill(s): Collecting and Organizing Data, Designing Projects and Investigations, Observing

Standards: Science (K–4)   Earth and Space Science A
             Science (5–8)   Earth and Space Science A, Life Science E

Activity 5: Arrangement and Storage

Thinking Skill(s): Collecting and Organizing Data, Classifying

Standards: Geography (K–4)   2.1
             Geography (5–8)   2.1
             Science (K–4)   Unifying Concepts and Processes A
             Science (5–8)   Unifying Concepts and Processes A, History and
                                    Nature of Science B

Activity 6: National Symbols

Thinking Skill(s): Collecting and Organizing Data, Interpreting

Standards: English   5, 12
             Geography (K–4)   3.1
             Geography (5–8)   3.1
             Social Studies (Early) 1c
             Social Studies (Middle) 1c

Activity 7: Detective Work

Thinking Skill(s): Collecting and Organizing Data, Classifying, Observing

Standards: Geography (K–4)   3.1, 4.1
Geography (5–8)   3.1, 4.1
Science (K–4)   Unifying Concepts and Processes A
Science (5–8)   Unifying Concepts and Processes A
Social Studies (Early)   3a, 3c
Social Studies (Middle)   3a, 3c

Activity 8:   What is This?

Thinking Skill(s): Collecting and Organizing Data, Criticizing, Decision Making

Standards: English   5, 6, 7, 8, 12
Science (5–8)   Science in Personal and Social Perspectives C, D

Activity 9:   Exploring Ecosystems

Thinking Skill(s): Collecting and Organizing Data, Observing, Design Projects and Investigations

Standards: Science (K–4)   Unifying Concepts and Processes D,
Life Science B, Earth Science A
Science (5–8)   Unifying Concepts and Processes D,
Life Science D, Earth Science A

Activity 10:   Flowering Plant Generalizations

Thinking Skill(s): Summarizing

Bugs

Students will research the names and function of various parts of a bug and will explore the different types of arthropoda. After exploring the characteristics of different bugs, students will create their own narratives about what it would be like to be a bug. In addition, students will chart the development and life cycle of a monarch and will track the migration patterns of the butterfly. The specific roles of bugs will be explored, such as that of the invader, the consumer, and the scavenger, and investigations of bug habitats will be conducted. At the end of this theme, students will create their own bug collection.

Activity 1:   Examine a Bug

Thinking Skill(s): Classifying, Observing

Standards: Science (K–4)   Unifying Concepts and Processes A, Life Science A
Science (5–8)   Unifying Concepts and Processes A, Life Science A

Activity 2:   **Let's Fly**

Thinking Skill(s): Applying Fact and Principles in a New Situation, Classifying, Collecting and Organizing Data, Comparing and Contrasting

Standards:	English	12
	Science (K–4)	Unifying Concepts and Processes A, D, E, Life Science A, C
	Science (5–8)	Unifying Concepts and Processes A, D, Life Science A, B, D, E
	Social Studies (Early)	3c
	Social Studies (Middle)	3c

Activity 3:   **Find the Right Letters**

Thinking Skill(s): Applying Facts and Principles in a New Situation, Collecting and Organizing Data

Standards:	English	5, 6, 12
	Science (K–4)	Life Science A, C
	Science (5–8)	Life Science A, B, C, D, E

Activity 4:   **Helpful or Harmful?**

Thinking Skill(s): Applying Facts and Principles in a New Situation, Classifying, Comparing and Contrasting

Standards:	English	7
	Science (K–4)	Life Science A, C
	Science (5–8)	Life Science A, D, Science in Personal and Social Perspectives C, D
	Social Studies (Early)	1a, 1b, 1d, 3h
	Social Studies (Middle)	1a, 1b, 1d

Activity 5:   **Growing Up**

Thinking Skill(s): Collecting and Organizing Data, Hypothesizing Observing

Standards:	Geography (K–4)	3.1
	Geography (5–8)	3.1
	Science (K–4)	Life Science A, B, C
	Science (5–8)	Life Science A, B, C, D
	Social Studies (Early)	3c
	Social Studies (Middle)	3c

Activity 6:   Open Your Eyes

Thinking Skill(s): Applying Fact and Principles in a New Situation,
                    Comparing and Contrasting, Observing

Standards: Science (K–4)   Life Science A, C, Science as Inquiry A
                    Science (5–8)   Life Science A, C, D, Science as Inquiry A

Activity 7:   Working Together

Thinking Skill(s): Comparing and Contrasting, Observing

Standards: Science (K–4)   Life Science A, C
                    Science (5–8)   Life Science A, C, D

Activity 8:   Collecting and Preserving

Thinking Skill(s): Classifying, Collecting and Organizing Data

Standards: English   5, 6, 12
                    Science (K–4)   Unifying Concepts and Processes A,
                                           Science as Inquiry A
                    Science (5–8)   Unifying Concepts and Processes A,
                                           Science as Inquiry A

Activity 9:   It Can't Be!

Thinking Skill(s): Imagining

Standards: English   5, 6, 12
                    Science (K–4)   Life Science A
                    Science (5–8)   Life Science A

Activity 10:   Bug Generalizations

Thinking Skill(s): Summarizing

Sports and Outdoor Activities

Students will explore the role of arousal in sporting events and will be able to practice those emotions during a role-play as a sports commentator. They will investigate the specialized types of equipment, tools, and supplies needed while participating in various sports and outdoor activities. Students will use trading cards to construct mental math activities and will acquire specialized terminology for sports. As students become familiar with various sports, they will be able to identify historical changes in the locations of teams, rules, equipment, and participants. In addition, students will design their own event schedule for a variety of sporting activities, plan their own mini-Olympics, and discover the impact that recreational activities can have on the environment.

Activity 1:   **Let's Pretend**

Thinking Skill(s): Looking for Assumptions, Observing

Standards: English   4, 12

Activity 2:   **This Looks Fishy**

Thinking Skill(s): Designing Projects or Investigations, Observing

Standards: English   6

Activity 3:   **Special Equipment**

Thinking Skill(s): Classifying

Standards: English   5, 6, 12

Activity 4:   **Mental Math**

Thinking Skill(s): Collecting and Organizing Data

Standards: Math   Compute Fluently (K–2, 3–5, 6–8)

Activity 5:   **Knowledge of the Game**

Thinking Skill(s): Classifying, Comparing and Contrasting

Standards: Social Studies (Early)   2b
                    Social Studies (Middle) 2b

Activity 6:   **If You Build It, They Will Come**

Thinking Skill(s): Classifying, Collecting and Organizing Data

Standards: Geography (K–4)   3.1
                    Geography (5–8)   3.1

Activity 7:   Event Schedules

Thinking Skill(s):   Collecting and Organizing Data, Classifying, Decision Making, Hypothesizing

Standards: Social Studies (Early)   2b
                   Social Studies (Middle)   2c

Activity 8:   Sports Time

Thinking Skill(s):   Collecting and Organizing Data, Interpreting, Observing

Standards: English   4, 5, 6, 12

Activity 9:   Leave No Trace

Thinking Skill(s):   Collecting and Organizing Data, Decision Making

Standards: Social Studies (Early)   3h
                   Social Studies (Middle)   3h

Activity 10:   Sports and Outdoor Activities Generalizations

Thinking Skill(s):   Summarizing

Parks and Forests

Students will investigate the various lands within the National Park System and the characteristics of each. As they learn about the park system, students will consider the natural resources available, the challenges the parks face (e.g., forest fires, logging, pollution, extinction, endangered and threatened species) and related controversial issues. Students will explore the interconnections among animals within the ecosystem from both the predator/prey and population density perspectives. Additional research will discuss the impact of urbanization and habitat fragmentation. Using the information gained in their study of parks and forests, students will design their own park or forest and identify how they will allocate their funds for spending. Students will have the opportunity to become an advocate for parks and forests and will create their own adventure story.

Activity 1:   This Land is Your Land

Thinking Skill(s): Classifying, Collecting and Organizing Data, Comparing and Contrasting, Decision Making

Standards: Geography (K–4)   2.1, 3.1
                Geography (5–8)   2.1, 2.2, 3.1
                Social Studies (Early) 3b, 3g, 3h
                Social Studies (Middle) 3b, 3h

Activity 2:   Keeping in Tune With Nature

Thinking Skill(s): Apply Facts and Principles in a New Situation,
                   Collecting and Organizing Data, Hypothesizing

Standards: English   4, 5, 6, 12

Activity 3:   On the Loose

Thinking Skill(s): Applying Facts and Principles in a New Situation,
                   Collecting and Organizing Data, Decision Making

Standards: Science (K–4)   Life Science C, Science in Personal
                                       and Social Perspectives D
                Science (5–8)   Life Science D, Science in Personal
                                       and Social Perspectives B

Activity 4:   Land Management

Thinking Skill(s): Collecting and Organizing Data, Hypothesizing

Standards: Geography (K–4)   2.1, 3.1
                Geography (5–8)   2.1, 2.2, 3.1
                Social Studies (Early) 3c, 6b, 6c
                Social Studies (Middle) 3c, 6c

Activity 5:   Setting Boundaries

Thinking Skill(s): Collecting and Organizing Data, Criticizing, Decision Making

Standards: English   7
                Science (K–4)   Science and Technology C, Science in Personal and
                                       Social Perspectives D
                Science (5–8)   Science in Personal and Social Perspectives B
                Social Studies (Early) 3h
                Social Studies (Middle) 3h

Activity 6: Environmental Design

Thinking Skill(s): Applying Facts and Principles in a New Situation, Collecting and Organizing Data

Standards:

English	5, 12
Geography (K–4)	2.1, 3.1
Geography (5–8)	2.1, 2.2, 3.1
Social Studies (Early)	6c
Social Studies (Middle)	6c

Activity 7: Adventure Stories

Thinking Skill(s): Classifying, Imagining

Standards:

English	4, 5, 6, 12

Activity 8: It's Debatable

Thinking Skill(s): Classifying, Collecting and Organizing Data, Criticizing, Decision Making

Standards:

English	7
Math	Compute Fluently (K–2, 3–5, 6–8)
Science (K–4)	Science in Personal and Social Perspectives D
Science (5–8)	Science in Personal and Social Perspectives B
Social Studies (Early)	3h, 3k, 5f
Social Studies (Middle)	3h, 3k, 5f

Activity 9: What a Resource

Thinking Skill(s): Collecting and Analyzing Data, Criticizing, Decision Making

Standards:

English	5, 12
Social Studies (Early)	3h, 9d, 9e
Social Studies (Middle)	3h, 9d, 9e

Activity 10: Parks and Forests Generalizations

Thinking Skill(s): Summarizing

Weather

In their study of weather, students will create their own classification system for weather-related terms, research the different ways weather data are collected, and investigate the urban legends involving the ability to sense weather changes. As they examine specific weather patterns, they will collect data from each of the different continents for 2 weeks and make predictions about upcoming weather events. In addition, students will identify how other cultures have adjusted their lifestyles to fit their environment. In order to get a better understanding of climates, students will construct a model that explains the various seasons and the relationship between the seasons and plant growth. They will also study the changes that occur during weather patterns as water shifts among solid, liquid, and gas states and the impact these states have on our ecosystem. At the end of this unit, students will write their own story that builds on historical evidence from a real-life natural disaster.

Activity 1: Weather Words

Thinking Skill(s): Applying Facts and Principles to a New Situation, Classifying, Collecting and Organizing Data, Decision Making

Standards:	English	8, 12
	Science (K–4)	Unifying Concepts and Principles A
	Science (5–8)	Unifying Concepts and Principles A

Activity 2: North Winds

Thinking Skill(s): Observing

Standards:	English	12

Activity 3: The Weather Today . . .

Thinking Skill(s): Collecting and Organizing Data, Comparing and Contrasting, Hypothesizing

Standards:	Science (K–4)	Unifying Concepts and Principles C, Science as Inquiry A
	Science (5–8)	Unifying Concepts and Principles C, Science as Inquiry A
	Social Studies (Early)	2b, 8a
	Social Studies (Middle)	2c

Activity 4: It Depends

Thinking Skill(s): Collecting and Organizing Data

Standards:	English	6, 12

Activity 5: Climate Patterns

Thinking Skill(s): Collecting and Organizing Data, Comparing and Contrasting, Hypothesizing

Standards:	Geography (K–4)	1.1, 3.2, 5.1
	Geography (5–8)	1.2, 3.1, 3.2, 5.1
	Science (K–4)	Earth and Space Science C
	Science (5–8)	Earth and Space Science A
	Social Studies (Early)	3c, 3f, 3g, 3h
	Social Studies (Middle)	3c, 3f, 3g, 3h

Activity 6:   Solid, Liquid, Gas

Thinking Skill(s): Collection and Organizing Data, Observing

Standards:	English	3, 4, 5, 12
	Science (K–4)	Earth and Space Science A, Physical Science A
	Science (5–8)	Physical Science A

Activity 7:   Down Came the Rain

Thinking Skill(s): Applying Facts and Principles to a New Situation, Collecting and Organizing Data, Observing

Standards:	Geography (K–4)	2.1, 4.1, 4.2, 4.3
	Geography (5–8)	2.1, 4.1, 4.2, 4.3
	Social Studies (Early)	3b, 3c
	Social Studies (Middle)	3b, 3c

Activity 8:   Rain, Rain, Go Away

Thinking Skill(s): Comparing and Contrasting, Observation

| Standards: | Science (K–4) | Earth and Space Science A, Physical Science A |
| | Science (5–8) | Physical Science A |

Activity 9:   Weather Writer

Thinking Skill(s): Collecting and Organizing Data, Criticizing, Decision Making, Summarizing

Standards:	English	3
	Geography (K–4)	5.1
	Geography (5–8)	5.1

Activity 10:   Weather Generalizations

Thinking Skill(s): Summarizing

Appendix 2:
Teacher Resources

American Forest Association. (1996). *The changing forest: Forest ecology*. Washington, DC: Author.

American Forest Association. (2000). *Project learning tree: Environmental education activity guide. Pre K–8* (7th ed.). Washington, DC: Author.

Bijlmakers, H. (2002). *Entomology for beginners*. Retrieved August 5, 2002, from the World Wide Web: http://www.bijlmakers.com/entomology/begin.htm.

Bernstein, L., Winkler, A., & Zierdt-Warshaw, L. (1996). *Environmental science: Ecology and human impact* (2nd ed.). New York: Addison-Wesley.

Council for Environmental Education. (2001). *Project WILD: K–12 curriculum and activity guide*. Houston, TX: Author.

Council for Environmental Education. (2001). *Project WILD aquatic: K–12 curriculum and activity guide*. Houston, TX: Author.

Doll, D. (2002). *Biospheres and ecospheres*. Retrieved September 14, 2002, from the World Wide Web: http://www.frii.com/~dboll/ecospher.htm.

EcoSphere R. *Enclosed ecosystems*. Retrieved September 14, 2002, from the World Wide Web: http://www.eco-sphere.com/ecospheres.html.

Earth-Life Web Productions. (2002). *Introduction to insect anatomy: What makes an insect an insect?* Retrieved August 5, 2002, from the World Wide Web: http://www.earthlife.net/insects/anatomy.html.

Elphick, C., Dunning, J. B., Jr., & Sibley, D. A. (Eds.). (2001). *National Audubon Society: The Sibley guide to bird life and behavior*. New York: Knopf.

Equipped to Survive TM. *Stay alive survival simulator*. Retrieved August 5, 2002, from the World Wide Web: http://equipped.com/stayalive/cgi-bin/sim/index.html.

Godwin, W. (2002). *Making an insect collection*. Retrieved August 5, 2002, from the World Wide Web: http://entowww.tamu.edu/collect1.html.

Hart, J. (1998). *Walking softly in the wilderness: The Sierra Club guide to backpacking*. San Francisco: Sierra Club Books.

Harvey, M. (1999). *The National Outdoor Leadership School's wilderness guide*. New York: Fireside.

Hoffman, M. P., & Frodsham, A. C. (1993). Natural enemies of vegetable insect pests. Ithaca, NY: Cooperative Extension, Cornell University. On Weeden, Shelton, Li, & Hoffman. (Eds.). (2002). *Biological control: A guide to natural enemies in North America*. Retrieved August 5, 2002, from the World Wide Web: http://www.nysaes.cornell.edu/ent/biocontrol/info/primer.html.

Jackman, J. A. (2002). *Identification of insect pests in gardens and ornamental plantings*. Retrieved August 5, 2002, from the World Wide Web: http://entowww.tamu.edu/academic/ucourses/ento489/material/insectid.html.

Larson, G. (1984). *The Far Side gallery*. New York: Andrews, McMeel & Palmer.

MacFarlane, R. B. (1985). *Collecting and preserving plants for science and pleasure*. New York: Arco.

Margulis, L., & Schwartz, K. V. (1998). *Five kingdoms: An illustrated guide to the phyla of life on Earth* (3rd ed.). New York: Freeman.

McGivney, A. (1998). *Leave No Trace: A guide to the new wilderness etiquette*. Seattle: The Mountaineers.

National Parks Conservation Association. (2002). *About NPCA*. Retrieved August 12, 2002, from the World Wide Web: http://www.eparks.org/about_ncpa.

National Parks Conservation Association. (2002). *Across the nation*. Retrieved August 12, 2002, from the World Wide Web: http://www.eparks.org/across_the_nation/visitor_experience.

National Parks Conservation Association. (2002). *A primer on federal lands*. Retrieved August 12, 2002, from the World Wide Web: http://www.eparks.org/about_ncpa/park_system/default.asp.

National Parks Conservation Association. (2002). *Cultural diversity*. Retrieved August 12, 2002, from the World Wide Web: http://www.eparks.org/cultural_diversity/native_expression/default.asp.

National Parks Conservation Association. (2002). *Marine and coastal*. Retrieved August 12, 2002, from the World Wide Web: http://www.eparks.org/marine_and_coastal/coral-reefs.

National Parks Conservation Association. (2002). *National park system units*. Retrieved August 12, 2002, from the World Wide Web: http://www.eparks.org/about_ncpa/park_system/a_to_c.asp.

National Parks Conservation Association. (2002). *Take action*. Retrieved August 12, 2002, from the World Wide Web: http://www.ncpa.org/take_action/park_planning/expert/default.asp.

National Parks Conservation Association. (2002). *Wildlife protection*. Retrieved August 12, 2002, from the World Wide Web: http://www.ncpa.org/wildlife_protection/threats.

National Register of Historic Places. (2002). *A guide for developing teaching with historic places lesson plans*. Retrieved August 12, 2002, from the World Wide Web: http://www.cr.nps.gov/nr/twhp/guide.htm.

National Register of Historic Places. (2002). *Teaching with historic places author's packet: Some sources of evidence*. Retrieved August 12, 2002, from the World Wide Web: http://www.cr.nps.gov/nr/twhp/source.htm.

Randall, G. (1998). *The Outward Bound map and compass handbook*. New York: Lyons Press.

Shanks, B. (1980). *Wilderness survival.* New York: Universe Books.

Smoky's Vault. (2002). *History of campaign.* Retrieved August 12, 2002, from the World Wide Web: http://www.smokeybear.com/vault/history.asp.

Some simple population models. (2002). Retrieved August 12, 2002, from the World Wide Web: http://www.west-bend.k12.ia.us/textbook/unit2/pop.html.

Texas Parks & Wildlife. *Safe, smart, survival.* Retrieved August 12, 2002, from the World Wide Web: http://tpwd.state.tx.us/adv/kidspage/survkit.htm.

United States Department of Agriculture (USDA) Forest Service. *Woodsy Owl welcome page.* Retrieved August 12, 2002, from the World Wide Web: http://www.symbols.gov/woodsy/woodsy.htm.

United States Department of Agriculture (USDA) Forest Service. *National trail system map.* Retrieved August 12, 2002, from the World Wide Web: http://www.fs.fed.us/maps.

United States Geological Survey (USGS). *National mapping information.* Retrieved September 14, 2002, from the World Wide Web: http://mapping.usgs.gov.

United States Geological Survey (USGS). *View USGS maps and aerial photo mages online.* Retrieved September 14, 2002, from the World Wide Web: http://mapping.usgs.gov/partners/viewonline.html.

United States Geological Survey (USGS). *Biological resources.* Retrieved September 14, 2002, from the World Wide Web: http://biology.usgs.gov.

Wade, C., & Tavris, C. (1996). *Psychology* (4th ed.). New York: HarperCollins.

Watercourse and the Council for Environmental Education. (1995). *Project WET: K–12 Curriculum and activity guide.* Bozeman, MT: Project WET.

Western Regional Environmental Education Council. (1995). *Taking action: An educator's guide to involving students in environmental action projects.* Bethesda, MD: Author.

Wong, J. (2000, November 22). *Animals regulate their numbers by own population density.* Retrieved August 12, 2002, from the World Wide Web: http://www.newsandevents.utoronto.ca/bin1/001122a.asp.

Appendix 3: Student Supplement—World Map

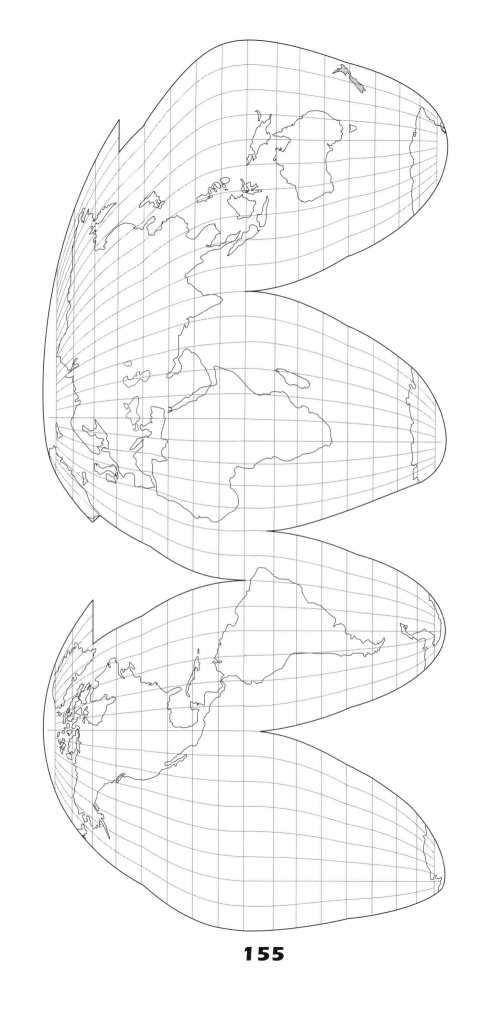

Appendix 5:
Answer Guide

The following answers are a guide to the activities. They do not represent a complete list of all possible answers, but rather are a starting point for further research and investigation.

Animals Activity 2: It's Time to Classify

Amphibians	Reptiles	Mammals	Birds	Fish
• live on land and water • breathe through skin and gills • lay eggs in water • are soft-skinned • are cold-blooded vertebrates • Frogs, toads, and salamanders are amphibians.	• have leathery scales • lay an amniote egg adapted to survival out of water • are cold-blooded vertebrates • most live on land, while some live in water • breathe through their lungs • Crocodiles, desert tortoises, and rattlesnakes are reptiles.	• can regulate their body temperatures • have hair or fur • except the duck-billed platypus and the spiny anteater, all mammals give birth to live young • produce milk via the pro mammary glands • breathe through their nostrils and lungs • are vertebrates • Elephants, bison, and wolves are mammals.	• are the only vertebrates with feathers • do not have teeth • have modified forelimbs (wings) • can regulate their body temperature • lay land-adapted eggs with shells • The blue jay, the owl, and the ostrich are birds.	• are cold-blooded vertebrates • have simple skeletons made of bone or cartilage • live in fresh water or sea water • have scales and fins • breathe with gills • The pike is a fish.

Animals Activity 4: Animal Antics

1.	milk	cow, goat
2.	stripes	zebra, coral snake
3.	mane	horse, zebra, mule, donkey
4.	pouch	kangaroo, opossum
5.	trunk	elephant
6.	wise	owl, elephant
7.	long neck	giraffe, ostrich
8.	America's bird	eagle
9.	laughing	hienna
10.	New York	buffalo
11.	man's best friend	dog
12.	carried mail	donkey, horse, pigeon

Animals Activity 7: "Oh, Give Me a Home"

Arctic:	Cold and frigid geographic region extending from the North Pole to the northern timberline.
Tundra:	Treeless region located between the ice cap and the tree line in arctic regions. The subsoil is permanently frozen and has low-growing vegetation (i.e., moss, lichens).
Semiarid highlands:	Area of light annual rainfall that can sustain only short grasses and plant life.
Taiga plains:	Subarctic evergreen forest area.
Sierras:	Rugged mountain range that is irregular in its formation.
Forest:	Dense growth of trees and other vegetation covering a large area.
Tropics:	Parallel lines of latitude 23 degrees and 27 minutes north and south of the equator that are the apparent limits of the direct rays of the sun. This area represents the boundaries of the torrid zone.
Mountains:	Region with high elevations.
Deserts:	Dry, barren, typically sandy region that can support little to no vegetation.
Temperate:	Two of the middle climate zones of the Earth lying between 23.5 and 66.5 degrees north and south of the equator.

Animals Activity 9: Baby Names

1.	bear	cub
2.	kangaroo	joey
3.	cat	kitten
4.	sheep	lamb
5.	dog	puppy
6.	deer	fawn
7.	horse	foal
8.	goose	gosling

Flowering Plants Activity 1: Flower Find

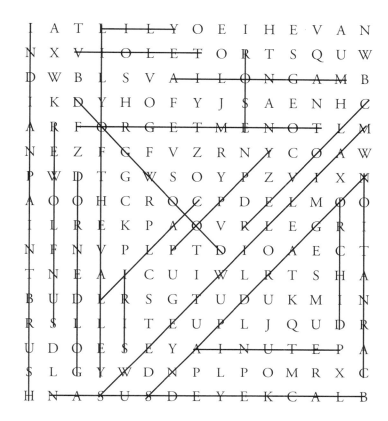

Flowering Plants Activity 2: A Flower's Parts

Stigma: the tip of the pistil of a flower in which pollen is placed during pollination

Peduncle: the stalk or stem that bears a solitary flower

Receptacle: the portion of the flower stalk that bears and holds the reproductive organs

Sepal: one of the green portions that forms the outer covering (the calyx) of a flower

Anther: organ at the tip of the stamen that expels pollen

Stamen: the reproductive organ of the flower that produces the pollen and usually consists of a filament and an anther

Perianth: the outer portion of the flower that contains the outer protective covering (the calyx) and the corolla

Filament: the slender stalk of a stamen that contains the anther

Ovary: the part of the pistil where seeds develop after fertilization (ovules)

Style: slender part of a pistil that rises from the ovary with the stigma on the tip

Corolla: fused or separated petals

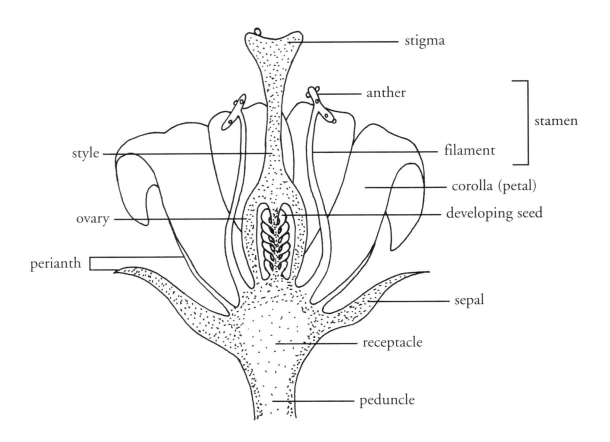

stigma

anther

stamen

style

filament

corolla (petal)

ovary

developing seed

perianth

sepal

receptacle

peduncle

Flowering Plants Activity 6: National Symbols

	State	Flower	Tree	Bird
1.	Maryland	black-eyed susan	white oak	Baltimore oriole
2.	Texas	bluebonnet	pecan	mockingbird
3.	Florida	orange blossom	cabbage palmetto	mockingbird
4.	Louisiana	magnolia	bald cypress	eastern brown pelican
5.	Tennessee	purple iris	yellow poplar	mockingbird
6.	Hawaii	hibiscus	kukui	nene
7.	Nebraska	goldenrod	cottonwood	western meadowlark
8.	Maine	pine cone and tassel	eastern white pine	chickadee
9.	California	golden poppy	blue spruce	lark bunting
10.	Minnesota	lady slipper	red pine	common loon

Flowering Plants Activity 8: What is This?

Poison ivy characteristics:
- grows as a climbing vine or as a nonclimbing shrub
- has three serrated-edge pointed leaves
- found in the East, Midwest, and South

Poison sumac characteristics:
- grows as a shrub or bush
- has two rows of 7–13 leaflets per branch
- lives in peat bogs and sandy swamps
- found in the North and South

Poison oak characteristics:
- has three leaves
- lives in sandy soil
- grows as a climbing vine, a small shrub, or as a standing shrub
- found in the Southeast and West

Bugs Activity 1: Examine a Bug

Abdomen:	the major endmost part of the body
Antennae:	flexible, jointed sensory appendage found on the head (typically found in pairs)
Claws:	a pincher-like structure at the end of a limb
Clypeus:	shield-like structure or plate on the front of the head of an insect
Compound eyes:	the eyes of most insects that consist of many light-sensitive elements that each form a portion of an image
Coxa:	the basal segment of the leg
Exoskeleton:	an external protective coating or structure of invertebrates
Femur:	the third segment of an insect's leg, typically that which is the thickest
Head:	the uppermost forward part of the body of both vertebrate and invertebrate organisms
Labrum:	a lip-like structure that forms the top of the mouth for many insects
Legs:	a limb or appendage used for support and movement
Mandible:	any of the insect's mouth parts
Maxillae:	laterally moving appendages located just behind the jaws
Scape:	the shaft of an insect's antennae
Spiracles:	openings in the exoskeleton of an insect or spider that allow for breathing
Tarsus:	a series of small segments on an insect's leg beyond the tibia
Thorax:	the second or middle region of the body that typically contains the legs and wings
Tibia:	the fourth segment of an insect's leg
Trochanter:	the segment of an insect's leg following the coxa

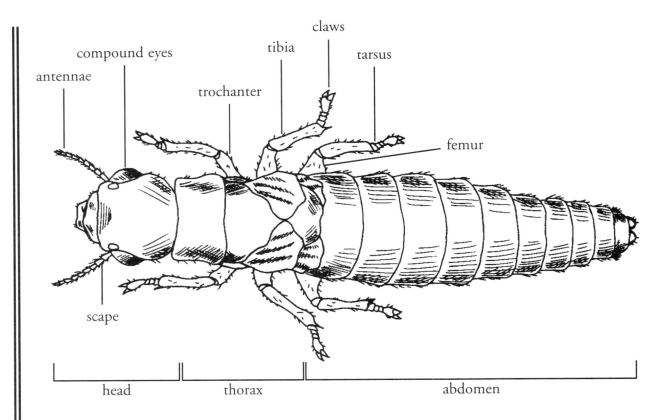

antennae

compound eyes

trochanter

tibia

claws

tarsus

femur

scape

head

thorax

abdomen

exoskeleton

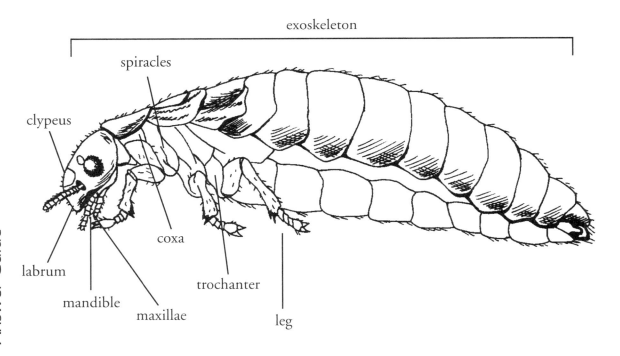

spiracles

clypeus

labrum

mandible

maxillae

coxa

trochanter

leg

Bugs Activity 2: Let's Fly

Bug Name	Insecta	Arachnida	Diplopoda	Chilopoda
ant	√			
antlion	√			
aphid	√			
boll weevil	√			
booklice	√			
butterfly	√			
cicada killer	√			
caddisflies	√			
carpenter bee	√			
centipede			√	
clothes moth	√			
cockroach	√			
cricket	√			
cut worm	√			
damselfly	√			
dragon fly	√			
earwig	√			
firebrat	√			
flea	√			
gnat	√			
grasshopper	√			
honey bee	√			
hornet	√			
katydid	√			
lace wing	√			
ladybird beetle	√			
leaf hopper	√			
louse	√			
mandit	√			
mayfly	√			
mealybug	√			
midge	√			
millipede				√
mite		√		
mosquito	√			
moth				
mud dauber	√			
pecan weevil	√			
psocid	√			
scale	√			
scorpion		√		

scorpion fly	√	
silverfish	√	
spider		√
springtail	√	
stonefly	√	
termite	√	
tick		√
thrip	√	
true fly	√	
walking stick	√	
white grub	√	
yellow jacket	√	

Bugs Activity 3: Find the Right Letters

1. butterfly
2. mosquito
3. grasshopper
4. flea

5. moth
6. wasp
7. cricket
8. ladybug

Bugs Activity 4: Helpful or Harmful?

Build webs to capture prey: spider, booklouse
Pests on animals and humans: tick, louse, thrip, gnat, mosquito, flea
Chew on books and household items: silverfish, cockroach, booklouse
Predators: tick, earwig, louse, true bug, beetle, gnat, true fly
Eat plants: grasshopper, walking stick, earwig, thrip, true bug, aphid, beetle, caterpillar
Structural pest: termite, beetle

Helpful: mandit, caddisfly, dragonfly, stonefly, mayfly, and scorpion fly

Sports Activity 2: This Looks Fishy

1. rod
2. reel
3. cast
4. lure
5. bait

6. bobber
7. hook
8. worm
9. fish
10. fly

Sports Activity 3: Special Equipment

1. goggles   swimming
2. hurdles   track
3. putter   golf
4. net   volleyball
5. paddle   canoeing
6. pebbles   hopscotch
7. beam   gymnastics
8. mallet   croquet
9. goal   soccer

Sports Activity 4: Mental Math

Example: 9 players + 3 strikes - 4 balls - 3 outs = 5

Sports Activity 5: Knowledge of the Game

Equipment	Maneuvers	Environment	People
bow	chute	boils	flotilla
dry bag	drop	clean	hole guide
gorp	ferry	current	keeper
life jacket	high side	eddy	paddle captain
paddle	portage	flow	river rat
stern	put-in	gradient	scout
throw bag	river left	haystack	swimmer
	river right	high water	trip leader
	run	hydraulics	
	swimmer's position	lateral	
	take-out	low water	
	wrap	pool drop	
		rapid	
		river rating	
		section	
		sieve	
		strainer	
		technical	
		volume	

Sports Activity 6: If You Build It, They Will Come

1. Orioles   Baltimore
2. Blue Jays   Toronto
3. Red Socks   Boston
4. Tigers   Detroit
5. Yankees   New York
6. Pirates   Pittsburgh
7. Cardinals   St. Louis
8. Royals   Kansas City
9. Reds   Cincinnati
10. Dodgers   Los Angeles

Parks and Forests Activity 1: This Land is Your Land

International historic site: see national historic site

National battlefield: a category including the following subcategories: national battlefield park, national battlefield site, national military park, and national memorial park.

National battlefield park: see national battlefield

National battlefield site: see national battlefield

National historical park: historic parks that are larger than a single property or building

National historic site: contains a single historical feature that was directly associated with an event or person

National lakeshore: established along the Great Lakes to preserve natural resources while providing opportunities for water-based recreation; can be established along any fresh-water lake

National monument: land owned or controlled by the government and authorized by the President as a landmark, structure, or other object of historical interest

National memorial: any location that commemorates a historic person or event (does not have to be historically related to the subject)

National military park: see national battlefield

National park: large national places that have a range of attributes, including significant historic assets (hunting, mining, and consumption of natural resources are not allowed)

National parkway: a roadway or parkland paralleling a road for scenic driving along a route containing a variety of cultural sites

National preserve: associated with national parks, but Congress allows public hunting, trapping, and oil/gas exploration and extraction

National reserve: area protected by local or state authorities in order to preserve the natural resources (hunting, fishing, and natural resource extraction may be permitted)

National river: a category including national river and recreation area, national scenic river, and wild and scenic river

National recreational area: provides outdoor water-based recreation for large numbers of people, typically around reservoirs

National seashore: established along the Atlantic, Gulf, and Pacific coasts ranging from primitive to developed beaches (hunting is allowed at many of these locations)

National trail: titles given to both the national scenic trails and national historic trails that extend more than 3,600 miles across the United States

Unit without designation: area under study by the national parks services

Wild and scenic river: see national river

Parks and Forests Activity 2: Keeping in Tune With Nature

Answers to all questions are true.

Weather Activity 2: North Winds

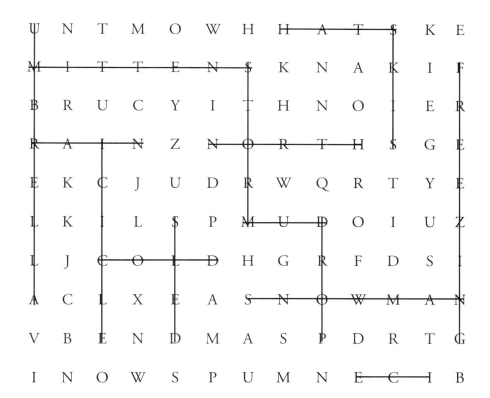

About the Author

Lindy T. Redmond, B.S., M.S., Elma, New York, is a teacher of children and adults. She has more than 30 years experience teaching all grades in elementary school, teaching parents of high-potential children, and training teachers in creative teaching strategies. Mrs. Redmond was instrumental in the development of a gifted and talented program in western New York and worked as a gifted programming catalyst. She has presented at conferences for New York State Advocacy for Gifted and Talented Education (AGATE) and the National Association for Gifted Children (NAGC). Mrs. Redmond has authored several books on creative thinking, creative writing, independent study, and creative product ideas for children.

She has been involved in creative problem solving competitions for 20 years. Mrs. Redmond is the Model School Program and Curriculum Consultant for Destination ImagiNation, an international creative problem solving program. For this organization, she is also an International Trainer, an Instant Challenge Regional and State Challenge Master, New York State board member, and an International Challenge Writer.

Lindy Redmond is a wife and mother of two sons.